NEIGHBORS WITH NO DOORS

The Truth about Homelessness, and How You Can Make a Difference

Ed,

Your creativity and passion to improve the lives of the unhoused in Paterson inspires me. I hope you enjoy my little book!

Much love,

Josiah

JOSIAH HAKEN

All photographs in this book copyright © by Corey Hayes 2021
Foreword copyright © by Detra Thomas 2022.

Neighbors with No Doors: The Truth about Homelessness and How You Can Make a Difference Copyright © by Josiah Haken 2022. All rights reserved. Published in the United States. No part of this book may be used or reproduced in any manner whatsoever without written permission except in the case of brief quotations embodied in critical articles and reviews.

Every effort has been made to obtain permission for pieces quoted or adapted in this work. If any required acknowledgements have been omitted, or any rights overlooked, it is unintentional. Please notify Josiah Haken of any omission, and it will be rectified in future editions.

Paperback ISBN 979-8-218-01705-7
E-book ISBN 979-8-218-01706-4

Cover design by Corey Hayes

Praise for Neighbors with No Doors

Neighbors with No Doors is a must read for anyone who wants to better understand the complexities of homelessness, and learn how each of us can positively impact the lives of those all around us who are often forgotten or ignored. Josiah Haken has helped so many people at Bombas thoughtfully engage with the unhoused community in New York City, and I am thrilled that everyone can now receive the benefit of his expertise, his many stories, and his wisdom.

— Dave Heath, Founder and CEO of Bombas

If you, like me, have ever walked by a homeless guy on the street and felt despair at how you could help, this book is for you. Josiah Haken has 10 years of hands-on, close-up experience on dealing with our neighbors without doors, and he busts stereotypes and offers real tools for individual action. Spoiler alert: there is something you can do. Every book claims to be practical and wise, but this one delivers.

— Belinda Luscombe, author and Editor at Large for TIME

Josiah Haken is a gifted storyteller and passionate advocate for our unhoused neighbors. In his book, *Neighbors with No Doors*, he shares very personal narratives from his 12 years serving at City Relief — from his early days as a volunteer to his newly appointed position as CEO. He provides the reader an intimate look at our most vulnerable population, and in doing so dispels some of the biggest myths surrounding homelessness.

At the very core of his book, he reminds us that our neighbors are human, just like us and we have a moral and civil responsibility to ensure basic human rights for all. My hope is that this book is the spark that ignites the fire for those who want to take action to help solve the homelessness crisis and are just not sure where to begin.

— Laura Ravo, Chief Operating Officer of Strand Books

Drawing on his years of experience, Josiah Haken shares one engaging story after another illustrating how thoroughly misguided many of our stereotypes about unhoused people are. In the process, he offers wise and practical advice on how each and every one of us can make a difference in the lives of homeless people. Everyone who cares about the plight of folks living on the street needs to read this book!

— Greg Boyd, author, theologian, and Pastor of Woodland Hills Church

Josiah Haken knows whereof he speaks. His passion and dedication to helping persons experiencing homelessness is evident in this book as he debunks the destructive myths we use to explain people who have lost it all (why else would one sleep on a sliver of cardboard in a snowstorm?). The leader of a fleet of mobile soup kitchens/help centers that stop around New York City and New Jersey, Haken educates the reader while telling fascinating stories of individuals whose humanity shines through the awful, gritty reality they endure.

— Dr. Deborah Padgett, Professor at the New York University Silver School of Social Work

In *Neighbors with No Doors*, Josiah Haken confronts many of the most common lies we've heard about our unhoused neighbors with the clarity, conviction, and compassion of the veteran New York relief leader that he is, complete with brutally honest stories and hard-won wisdom. Not only does Haken dispel the myths that homeless people are more lazy, more dangerous, more mentally ill, and more drug addicted than the rest of us, he also addresses many of the most common fears that hold us back from helping more. By telling us about mistakes he's made, Haken shows that you don't have to be an expert to make a difference in a person's life. And by giving us respectful methods to engage, he empowers us to love our unhoused neighbors in ways we may have thought impossible. This book is concise yet has room to draw readers in through its stories. It's also practical, with accessible on-ramps for readers to get started serving right away in our own contexts. Both a well-researched field guide and an inspiring testimony, Haken has written an essential work on homelessness that meets the moment.

— T. C. Moore, Lead Pastor at Roots Covenant Church

Neighbors With No Doors is a compassionately argued and remarkably accessible contribution to the conversation about homelessness. It's a great tool for housed neighbors who may not know where to start.

— Sara Newman, Director of Organizing for the Open Hearts Initiative

At the stop light, on the sidewalk, or riding on the train, we are confronted with the needs of unhoused people all around us. So what do we do? Josiah Haken answers that question with stories, statistics, and experiences that connect our desires for a more just and loving world with practical steps to bring that world into existence.

— Jonathan Walton, author, Partner at KTF Press, and Senior Resource Specialist for Intervarsity USA

In his powerful debut, *Neighbors With No Doors*, Josiah Haken helps us all reimagine solutions to homelessness by debunking the myths that the unhoused are just lazy, dangerous, mentally ill, or drug addicted. A true practical visionary, he shares his decades of personal stories and data-based insights to give us, first, a new lens to see from, and second, tools to take personal action. If you are ready to drop old beliefs in the most efficient way possible, and step into your next level of understanding and engagement, this book is for you!

— Susanne Conrad, mother, author, and Founder of Lightyear.co

I have heard it said that if you want to consider yourself an ally to a particular group of people, you better be standing close enough to get hit with the stones that are thrown at them. I can tell you from our working relationship and from the time we spent in the trenches together, Josiah Haken has gotten pegged with more than his fair share of stones. Homelessness statistics and practical advice are great, and this book has them in spades. But if you really want trustworthy directions, listen to the guy who has walked the road a million times. Read. This. Book.

— Reverend Jeff Cook, writer and former Outreach Leader for City Relief

Neighbors With No Doors is the down-to-earth guide we all need as we spend time on the streets loving and caring for our unhoused neighbors. With years of experience, sacrifice, and wisdom under his belt, Josiah reminds us that each one of these precious humans has a beautiful story to tell, so much to offer the world, and a meaningful future ahead of them.

— Nick Laparra, podcaster, speaker, and writer

I love this book because I hate the powerlessness I feel when I see the many unhoused people in my community—especially when I see them outside in our cold Minnesota winters! We all want our neighbors to have shelter. But the problem overwhelms us in size, and it's hard to know what to do in particular situations where we could actually make a positive difference. Josiah gives us a concise, entertaining, motivating, and informative guide that can help us do our part in bringing good to bad circumstances. After reading this book I feel empowered! Thank you, Josiah!

— Dan Kent, author and pastor

Up until my mid twenties I judged people living on the streets. I had the typical stereotypes, thinking that people were lazy or that they simply wanted to be homeless. Josiah Haken's book is something I wish I'd read back then. It would have been an eye opener for me. His reflections aren't merely opinion. They are rooted in the type of knowledge that only comes through experience. At the end of the day, people want to be seen as people; Josiah helps us understand that.

— Bob Dalton, podcaster and founder of Sackcloth & Ashes

Josiah Haken gives readers insight into the complex issues facing those who are experiencing homelessness. In addition, he gives practical advice on how we can help bring dignity to our friends on the street.

— Mike Polster, Missions Pastor at Northview Church

Do you want to be a better neighbor? That is the simple question that Josiah Haken is asking us as we consider serving unhoused people in our world. Josiah, in his disarming, engaging way, provides a myriad of actionable tips to help us become smart, confident advocates. With absorbing storytelling, he dismantles the stigmas, lies, and narratives that can hold us back from effectively caring for people experiencing homelessness. If you are serious about wanting to be a better neighbor, read this!

— Dave Rodriguez, CEO of Destinyworks, LLC

What a joy to read! This book takes you on a journey — one that's engaging and compelling. Josiah Haken's passion for our homeless friends is contagious, informed, and insightful. I found myself wanting to learn even more. Thank you, Josiah, for helping us to see our friends more clearly — for sharing personal stories so we can have more compassion and insight into mankind. We can all make a difference if we just have the right tools, and I will be recommending this book as a valuable resource for everyone who looks to serve this overlooked community!

— John McKinzie, Lead Pastor of Hope Fellowship

Many people are bewildered, wanting to help our homeless neighbors but not having the first clue how to do so. I often struggle to know where to send them for answers. But I will now point them toward this book. Packed with humane stories about homelessness, *Neighbors with No Doors* addresses stereotypes head-on. It is neither fluffy nor propaganda — it's real. And it will challenge your understanding of homelessness while at the same time providing compelling and tangible action steps.

— Josh Dean, Executive Director of Human.nyc

For all my unhoused friends
who let me in to their lives, with gratitude.

Table of Contents

Foreword 1
Introduction 7
Lies about Laziness 27
Lies about Danger 45
Lies about Mental Health 61
Lies about Drug Use 71
Engaging Neighbors with Compassion 89
Going Further 99
Building Community 111
Bringing It Home 121
My Neighbors 125
Acknowledgments 147

Foreword

Homelessness. For many of us, just reading the word produces unpleasant images and our inner selves recoil. Seeing a homeless person can cause us to quickly change our intended route to avoid the possibility of making eye contact with someone we have not prepared for and do not understand. Many times we write the story of the person we are avoiding, and the tale makes them the responsible party who got what they deserved.

Once, our family was going to a conference in Dallas, Tx. We were driving downtown in our 15-passenger van. You may think that is an interesting choice for a family vehicle, but we had seven children and we were traveling across 16 states doing what folks in the church world call "revivals" as a ministry for families. We passed many men and women sleeping on strips of cardboard, a pitiful barrier between their bodies and the burning heat of the sidewalk on that summer day. It made my heart squeeze in pain. I pointed them out to my children and explained that is what happens to people who do not follow the ways of God and choose instead to fall into a sinful lifestyle.

Years later, as I stood in line in New York City waiting for my own homeless shelter to open, I don't know what story those passing me on the sidewalk composed in their heads. But I guessed it was not one of kindness. I'm not sure the people of New York would call it sin, but they probably assumed I was leading a life of laziness and bad habits. It was difficult to stand there and feel the disdain that came from the slight shaking of their heads or quick glances away from the line of us women biding our time until we could check in. Until we could begin our evening routine of walking in single-file lines with escorts to the room that held 15 sets of bunk beds, getting our belongings settled in the huge cage that held the one suitcase we were each allowed, and grabbing our clear bag of toiletries for our timed ten-minute shower. It was like a prison. I lost 24 pounds in the four months I spent in the shelter. I couldn't get food that fit my allergy needs, and anyway, I lost my appetite.

If I had known my stay in the shelter would only be four months, it would have been much easier to navigate. But when I entered through the front door on October 31, 2016, infinity stretched out before me, and I was terrified.

I'm from Arkansas. I was a pastor's daughter and then a pastor's wife for a total of 54 years. I was born and raised in an ultra-conservative Baptist group that believed women were born to serve men, produce children, and run homes in a manner that brings glory to God. As a girl, I was drawn charts depicting how I had to stay under the authority of a man, whether it was my dad or husband, to have the blessing and protection of God. I learned to ask for the permission and blessing from those authorities before I did anything outside my house. I did that gladly.

Long story short, I was married three weeks and knew I wanted out, but you don't walk away from that world. You can't. I stayed 34 years in that relationship. I told no one that I was miserable, firmly believing that my love and forgiveness would allow him to see his emotional cruelty and love me.

After 32 years of this, with thoughts of suicide pounding in my brain, I went to a counselor who had helped me through some childhood trauma and told her I needed to talk about my marriage. Eventually, she asked me, "If he was beating you, would you leave him?" I answered, "Of course, I would. I know that is wrong!" Her next words were like a telephoto lens bringing my situation into sharp focus and I immediately felt their truth and their pain. "What he has done to you is worse than beating the crap out of you every day." My invisible bruises pulsated with the pain his passive-aggressive and frankly sociopathic behavior had caused.

Fast forward a year-and-a-half. I had brought in an interventionist and a mediator, who were both originally horrified at his behavior, but ultimately fell prey to the same charms I had. I knew I had to get out before I died from stress or gave up and did the unthinkable out of sheer despair.

He and I were driving down the interstate heading home to Fort Smith from Clarksville in Arkansas, and he said one of his charming, accusatory remarks about something I had done. He wanted to bring me back in line under his authority. But I had been doing research on his type of behavior. I had come to the realization that I was not helping by being submissive and forgiving, but rather I was enabling a man who had no business pastoring or leading anyone, let alone me. He uttered his remark, something inside me snapped, and words came out of me that surprised us both. "You're a son of a bitch!" He pulled over to the side of the interstate, and got in my face with his finger, yelling at me. I felt something inside telling me it was time. I got my purse, opened the door, stepped out and started walking down the interstate. A car pulled over and picked me up.

My oldest son helped me in what I have come to call my escape. He brought me to New York to stay with him and his wife for a few weeks. It turned into a year. When they moved out of state because of a job transfer, I stayed in New York. My other son urged me to come live with him, but that would mean moving back to the epicenter of all the trouble, and I knew it would put me back in the same emotional trap.

I made it a couple of months in New York with the help of friends who rented me a room cheap. They told me it was temporary because they had family coming in, but wanted to keep me out of the city shelters. They did accomplish that, for a while anyway. But after a thorough search, I knew I could not afford anything else available. That's how I ended up standing in line at the women's shelter.

I exhausted every avenue searching for assistance, and finally a friend put me in touch with a man who she told me helps the homeless. I arrived at our meeting late. I was disheveled and sweaty from nerves, getting lost, and the heat. I was dreading telling this man why I needed help. I had been through multiple screenings for services by this point. The questions were extremely personal and emotionally difficult to answer. And so far, these types of meetings had not resulted in me finding helpful services. They had only drained my confidence.

I sat and looked down at my hands trying to get a measure of control over my emotions. But when I looked up into the eyes of the man across from me, my heart was put at ease by his kind eyes, his smile, and his spirit of love. There was not one ounce of judgement. Instead he extended grace, listened with openness, and treated me with dignity. By the time we were done, I was calm and hopeful.

Josiah Haken and his team helped me navigate the worst time of my life. Did that make it easy? No, but I had a support system, encouragement, guidance, and love. That made my time doable. And none of those things went away when I found a home.

I like to think of Josiah as a door that swings easily both ways. There is no pushing hard only to realize the sign says, "Pull." If you are homeless, you experience Josiah as a door to resources, services, kindness, and even a friend. If you have never experienced homelessness, or if you look down on people who have, Josiah is a door that lets you enter the real world gently. He helps you learn, see, and know that one size does not fit all when it comes to the stories of the homeless. He opens his heart and shares the real stories of people who fall into homelessness for reasons beyond their control. Or he explains how some make choices that put them into a hamster wheel of policies and circumstances which keep them from being able to find stability. He is a door through which the homeless find a meal, warm socks, toiletries, rehab, shelter for the night, or just a smile, a hug, or a listening ear.

Josiah is not a door that makes you stop in your tracks and wonder what is on the other side. He's not ornate or pretentious. He is a door that gives you a sense of safety, peace, and hope, like the front door of your home

I hope you decide to walk through the door he is showing you with this book. His experiences, his life, and his love for those who live without an address are powerful. If you walk through, you will not be the same. Your heart will experience

NEIGHBORS WITH NO DOORS

a change that may lead to great things. Like the next time you see a homeless individual, you don't alter your steps. You don't tell yourself a story. Maybe you instead offer a look, a nod, a smile, a friend.

Detra Thomas

Introduction

Maliq is one of the first people I met with no place to call home. I was volunteering for the first time with City Relief, a nonprofit organization that connects people experiencing homelessness to services in New York City and New Jersey. We were in East Harlem by the Metro North train station. Maliq stood against a chain link fence separating the sidewalk from a small grassy lot with signs warning potential trespassers of rat poison. He was tall, broad, and his tank top revealed sculpted muscles

"I told him, 'f*ck you, I'm not paying for my own backpack! You stole that from me while I was sleeping, you piece of sh*t!'" Maliq was telling me a story about his experience sleeping in a New York City shelter a few nights before.

"So how did he respond?" I asked.

"He said that he bought my bag from another guy in the shelter two hours earlier and since it was mine he'd let me have it for half of what he paid!" He paused for emphasis, building up to the punchline, which he delivered with effortless charisma. "So I told him, since he was willing to sell me my own bag for half price, I'd be willing to kick the sh*t out of him for half the time. Or he could just give me back my f*ckin' bag and I'd let him walk away for free!" We both laughed out loud.

"I'm going for another cup of soup, do you want anything? Lemonade? Bread?" I gestured toward the retrofitted school bus turned outreach vehicle that City Relief affectionately calls the "relief bus."

"No, I'm good." His eyes traveled from the food service window on the side of the bus to the block lettering that advertised the kind of services and programs to which City Relief could connect people. "So what kind of programs do you guys offer?"

"We do a bunch of stuff. But honestly I'm pretty new." I decided that wasn't quite honest enough so I added, "Okay, I'm extremely new. I don't have a clue what we can do to help, but I can find out for you." I was 24 years old at the time. I had never been homeless. And that day was maybe the fifth or sixth time I had ever set foot in New York City, let alone spent any time talking to someone on the streets of East Harlem. I didn't have the foggiest clue what a shelter looked or smelled like. I had never used drugs, unless you count drinking a few Yuenglings my older brother brought to my apartment the night before I married my wife at the age of 19. I grew up in a stable, albeit adventurous household. I'm the youngest of four children and one of three who were born in Africa. I felt completely inadequate to help Maliq in any significant way, but I was determined to try.

"What kind of help are you looking for?"

"I drink too much. I always have. I had a good job, but I lost it. Now I'm back on the streets and I'm tired." His transparency was surprising. Most of the people I know don't open up to people they just met about their struggles with alcohol. When I first started working with the unhoused community,

INTRODUCTION

I assumed that in order for me to effectively "help" someone in the street I would have to spend a lot of time learning about their experiences first. And I thought I'd have to earn some street cred before anyone would talk to me about their challenges. I figured my white skin, youth, and obvious ignorance would be a neon sign reading "I can't help you, so don't bother asking."

"Well, let me get the outreach leader and see what can be done. Don't go anywhere." I scanned the crowd looking for the staff member who drove the bus to East Harlem from the base of operations in Elizabeth, New Jersey where the relief buses sit overnight and the volunteers and staff cook our world famous soup. I spotted him by the tables that were set up for volunteers and guests to sit down and enjoy a meal together. A self-described hillbilly, Austin wore a fisherman's cap and had an outstanding beard. I met him for the first time at a fundraiser for City Relief. He definitely carried himself more confidently in the streets than he did over a fancy meal with a suit and tie. I spent the entire fundraiser trying to decide if he was stoned or just uncomfortable. I liked him instantly. I jogged over and got his attention. We walked back to Maliq and I introduced the two of them.

"Maliq, this is Austin. He has been doing this for over five years and definitely knows more about the resources for folks in New York City than I do." Maliq nodded his approval.

"So what's going on, man? How can we help you?" Austin got right to the point. Maliq called his directness and raised him with some honesty.

"I need to detox from alcohol."

"You got insurance? Medicaid? ID?"

"Yeah, I got all that."

"You want to go today?"

"Yeah." As he said it, Maliq took another bite of the vegetable soup he was picking at with seeming disinterest.

Austin pulled out his phone. "Let's see your benefits card." Maliq put the soup down on the sidewalk and started rummaging through his pockets. He pulled out a plastic card with his picture and some official-looking, blue writing. "Alright, hold on." Austin took the card and dialed a number before starting to walk away, leaving Maliq and I to continue our conversation. I asked Maliq how he stayed so fit. He told me about how he worked out in the park every single day. He was explaining his workout routine with meticulous detail when Austin returned.

"Well, I've got good news and bad news. The good news is that your Medicaid is all set and someone from the detox is on his way to pick you up. The bad news is they are all the way across town and won't get here for an hour."

"That's not so bad," I said with the confidence of someone who'd been working on the streets for all of five minutes. "We can hang out until they get here." But Maliq was not so sure.

"Okay. That's fine. But I need to run and get something quick. I'll be right back." He turned and walked away. His long stride carried him up the sidewalk toward the Metro North train station. His abrupt departure had me concerned. He was clearly on a mission but it almost felt like we had done something to offend him. He said he would be right back, but I wasn't convinced. I looked at Austin.

"What should we do?" I asked.

"Nothing we can do but wait." I did, but I was anxious. I started to replay our conversation up to that point in my

INTRODUCTION

head and I couldn't figure out if there was something I should have done differently. Should I have asked him what he needed? Should I have suggested that I go with him? Should I have tried to convince him to stay? Maliq was gone for a long time. When 15 minutes turned to 30 I began to give up hope. But then, out of nowhere, there he was. Walking back significantly more slowly than he had walked away. He carried a paper bag that he didn't have when he left.

"Dude! I thought you ditched us!"

"No, man, I just needed something. If I'm going to detox, I might as well have one last beer ... or two." He smiled as he pulled out one of the two beer cans he had hidden tightly in a brown paper disguise. He cracked the aluminum lid back off the top of the first one.

"I get that." I had no problem with him drinking away the last half hour before the detox driver showed up, especially if it meant he would actually be there to get his ride to the rehab program.

"So, when did you start drinking?" I asked.

"When I was 13 years old."

"Thirteen?" I asked incredulously.

"Yep. My mom drank and all her boyfriends drank. So one day I was in our apartment and she left me with one of her boyfriends who gave me a beer. He told me I was ready to be a man. I never looked back."

"So what happened to the boyfriend?"

"He hit my mom so I punched him in the face. Man, did he beat the sh*t out of me all the time! My mom begged him to stop, but he told her he was teaching me to be a man. Apparently I had a lot to learn. Eventually I got bigger and our fights weren't quite so one-sided. I guess he didn't like getting hit back, so he told my mom she had to choose: me or him. She chose him. I had to leave. I've been on the streets ever since." He took another long sip of his beer.

The flatness of his voice hit me like a truck. I wasn't able to reconcile the tragedy of his childhood with the matter of fact tone he used to describe it to me. I imagined the pain of being rejected by one of the people we expect to care for him the most: his mother. How could she do that? What would lead her to choose her boyfriend over her own son? I was angry on his behalf. Why wasn't he? I would have expected tears, cursing, something.

All of a sudden I remembered where I was. The noise of friends, both homeless and not, having conversations around us mingled with the shake of the train thundering over our heads on Park Avenue. The sun was bright. There weren't any clouds to speak of. It was a warm October day, and from the way he told me the story of his life, he could have been reading from a newspaper. The only visible evidence of the trauma he suffered as a kid was the paper bag collecting condensation from the beer cans.

Maliq finished his second beer in two swallows. "I need another beer." In an instant my empathy was drowned by frustration.

"Dude, you're almost there! Your ride will be here any second! Don't go!" I pleaded.

"I need to go get some money and then I'll be right back."

"The detox driver will be here any minute. Please don't go." He left. Again. He disappeared around the corner and about 10 minutes later a silver minivan pulled up to the curb. A man with a lanyard got out and walked toward Austin, who shook his head and pointed in the direction of where Maliq had turned the corner. The driver agreed to hang around for a few minutes and have a cup of soup in case Maliq returned. The outreach was over, so we started wiping down the tables and carrying them to the back of the City Relief bus. Hope was draining out of me fast. The detox driver finished his soup, shook hands with Austin, and started to climb back into his van. Just as he started the engine, I heard a familiar voice from around the corner, "Wait!" I ran to the van and knocked on the window before the driver could pull away.

"Wait! He's here! He's here!"

Maliq was jogging in our direction with a new paper bag clutched in his right hand. The detox driver rolled down his window and looked at the bag and back to Maliq. "You can't bring that with you."

"No problem." Maliq cracked open the beer, chugged it in seconds, and climbed into the van.

I never saw Maliq again. It has been over a decade since that interaction and I have spoken to hundreds of men and women experiencing homelessness since, but his story sticks with me. Whenever I hear people talk about how homeless folks are just lazy, I think of how disciplined Maliq was with his daily workout routine and how hard he worked to stay presentable. When people dismiss homeless people as mentally ill or chemically dependent, I wonder how I would have responded to being rejected by my mother for a man who repeatedly beat me. Whenever I hear people complain about the dangers of having homeless people in their neighborhoods, I remember how Maliq welcomed me into his life with open arms.

I believe that in order for us to collectively address the issue of homelessness, we need to start by changing the narratives we tell about the individuals who experience it. "Homeless" is not a state of being. People *experience* homelessness, and people are not an *issue*. They are not a political talking point. They are not a "blight" or an "eyesore." I don't believe anyone should be defined by their living situation. These are mothers, fathers, sons, daughters, friends, and neighbors. They are college students, war veterans, athletes, mechanics, teachers, and musicians. They are survivors. They are contributors. They are human beings with intrinsic value and dignity. Consequently, throughout this book I will use different terms to describe the housing situation of the people that I've met along the way. Sometimes I will use the term "homeless" because that's the term that many of my friends use to describe themselves. Other times I will use words like "unhoused" or "living on the street." The diversity of my word choice reflects the complexity of each individual's circumstances. Defining an entire population with a generic and overused label only reinforces the stigma that needs to be dismantled.

I grew up with missionary parents in the West African country of Cameroon. While people don't typically go into mission work in developing countries for the money, pretty much any American living in Cameroon is wealthier than almost everyone else in the neighborhood. And our family was no exception. We lived in a simple house constructed of cement cinder blocks, tile floors, and a tin roof. My two brothers and I shared a bedroom and a bathroom because, as the only girl in the family, my sister got her own space. We had a big yard with six mango trees, two guava trees, and an avocado tree that

INTRODUCTION

dropped fruit onto the tin roof with such loud bangs that we would wake up in a panic. Our home was enclosed by a matching cinder block wall with broken beer bottles from the local brewery cemented on top to discourage people from trying to climb over. There was a metal gate that would open up to reveal a short stone driveway where we parked our beat up, mostly white Toyota van. There wasn't really anything worth watching on our ancient TV that only received two channels, so most evenings my family and I would sit and talk around our black, octagon-shaped kitchen table at dinner time. Occasionally the sound of a rock banging against our gate out front followed by the quiet sound of a Cameroonian child saying, "J'ai faim" ("I'm hungry") would puncture our conversation. My mom would quietly get up from the table, get out a baguette, slice it in half, fill it with ham and cheese, and walk it out to the boy. It wasn't uncommon for people around us to ask for help. It was normal to have children follow us around the neighborhood asking for leftovers or used clothing. There was so much poverty that my family could never solve all the problems. But while I'm sure it felt like a drop in the ocean to give one hungry child a sandwich, I remember my parents taking turns making an effort to help one person at a time.

Every couple of years my parents would bring us back to central Pennsylvania so they could connect with churches and donors who supported their work, and we eventually moved back "home" permanently to Hershey, Pennsylvania when I was 14 years old. I graduated high school in 2004 and began my new life in the wealthiest country in the world. The first step was to marry my girlfriend. Next, I got a job bartending at a steakhouse nearby, but I didn't think that would be enough to provide for my new wife, who was a nursing student at the time. I managed to snag a job giving estimates for kitchen remodeling projects and started plugging away at the "American dream." The plan was for me to pay the bills while my wife went to school, then we would trade. The problem was that nobody taught us how to manage money, so we were spending it as fast as we were making it. When she graduated, she took a job in the ICU and I kept helping people choose what kind of edge profiles they wanted for their granite countertops.

In December of 2009, my wife and I moved to New Jersey. For six months we learned the hard way that the closer one moves to New York City, the more expensive it is to survive. I was not making nearly enough money (now at a Starbucks) to supplement my wife's income and pay the rent. We got behind on our bills and debt collectors started coming after us on a regular basis. I changed the ringtone on my cellphone to something more melodic and soothing so I wouldn't panic when I got calls from collection agencies.

Around the same time, I discovered a soup kitchen in New Brunswick and decided that volunteering to wash dishes was a better use of my time than sitting around doing nothing after my shift of steaming milk and pouring espresso shots. I watched the guests as they returned their trays, and I thought about how I wasn't too far away from being one of them.

A few months later, one of the pastors at the church we were attending invited me to a banquet to raise money for an organization that helped homeless folks in New York City and New Jersey. I thought it was ironic that somebody decided that I should attend a fundraiser, considering my negative bank account and the list of missed calls from collection agencies on

INTRODUCTION

my cell phone. Maybe my reputation as a first-class dishwasher was spreading and they were looking to offer me a job. In hopes of getting a free beer out of the deal, I accepted the invitation. The banquet was for City Relief. This is the same faith-based nonprofit organization I was volunteering with when I met Maliq. It's also the organization where I'm now the CEO. City Relief takes retrofitted school buses and other outreach vehicles into urban areas with large homeless populations to offer a free meal, friendship, and connections to services like shelters, employment training programs, and public benefits. We mobilize thousands of volunteers every year and believe that every person experiencing homelessness bears the image of God, and therefore has unsurpassable value which makes serving them an honor and a privilege.

I volunteered with City Relief one time and quickly realized that serving on the streets was very different from washing dishes in a soup kitchen. The model of outreach was much more hands-on. By setting up tables and chairs for our guests to eat on the sidewalks, City Relief creates a vibe that feels like a street fair or a block party. We bring canopies for shade when it's bright and protection when it rains. We clean up after ourselves well and we make sure that we have enough volunteers to do more than just distribution. Our volunteers sit and enjoy the same meals that we serve to our guests. We want everyone to experience excellent customer service and compassion regardless of their income or housing situation.

I was hooked. It didn't take long for me to volunteer in every community that City Relief serves. Some of them reminded me of where I grew up. In East Harlem, for example, we parked right in front of an African hair braiding salon. The women wore brightly colored clothing and head coverings and sat on plastic chairs out front. They were highly entertained when a 24-year-old white kid wandered over and ask them in thick Cameroonian French if they wanted anything. They yelled to their friends in the salon to come outside and get some bread before we left. Everywhere we went, there were beautiful people speaking different languages and connecting over a meal. I quickly realized that this model of outreach—starting with compassion and then creating connections to services—was a perfect fit for my personality and my experience.

I kept showing up at City Relief until they hired me full time as an Outreach Leader. Honestly, I felt pretty inadequate for the first year. I had no personal history with homelessness, addiction, or relationship trauma so I often felt like I didn't have anything to offer our guests. But I did have enough cross-cultural experience to know what I did *not* know. And I received a crash course in the challenges our guests experienced as they survived without adequate housing, employment, or social networks. I learned about public benefits in New York City and how one could access things like the Supplemental Nutrition Assistance Program, colloquially called "food stamps," or government sponsored medical insurance for low-income residents called Medicaid. I learned about Social Security benefits and 2010E housing applications. Most importantly, I learned how building trust was the best way to maintain credibility with a population of people who are too often forgotten and overlooked.

I also experienced the vicarious frustration of witnessing the endless series of logistical problems homeless folks face. How do people with no address receive mail? How do people with no job get a home to have an address? How does someone with no address, phone number, or ID land a job? How do you acquire an ID when you have no other documentation? How do people with no bathroom get ready for an interview? I saw unhoused people get turned away for services because they didn't get in the right line at the right time. At the same outreach location where I met Maliq, I met a guy named Jason with brain trauma and epilepsy who regularly went without medication because whenever he had a seizure on the sidewalk or in his shelter, his medicine bottle was stolen, and his Medicaid would only cover one prescription per month.

I met so many people who were forced to choose between the possibility of improving their lives for the long haul or risking their survival today. One woman named Cindy had to choose between keeping her apartment or being fully present for her daughter. Cindy's disability check was directly linked to her continued use of a medication that made her sleep through most of the afternoon. If she stopped taking the medication or cut back on the dosage, she would no longer qualify for the amount of rental assistance she received. I was heartbroken to hear the anguish in her voice as she described how badly she wanted to be more awake and present for her little girl after school. But she was scared to death of losing her benefits and being forced back into the municipal shelter system.

I witnessed the black-and-white, in-or-out rules and regulations in the shelters themselves that sometimes forced families apart while trying to keep them safe. More than once, I encountered men who couldn't live with their families in a public shelter, because in a moment of anger and frustration, they punched a wall or raised their voice and a security guard reported it as a "domestic violence incident." This would instantly trigger a forced separation while the event itself was investigated, requiring the father to defend himself while taking care of his family from afar and navigating the bureaucracy of his new life in a single men's shelter.

I watched as some people were turned away from services they needed simply because their traumatic circumstances had brought them to the edge of despair, so they struggled to communicate without yelling in frustration or using coarse language. I sat on the phone with homeless guests as they tried again and again to get help in a shelter system that seemed at best disinterested, and at worst antagonistic toward them. I never planned on spending thousands of hours wrestling with the difficulties of homelessness, but the longer I stayed, the more passionate I became.

Another aspect of my job, besides directly helping and advocating for my homeless neighbors, is leading volunteers into the streets to help them build their own relationships with our guests. As a Christian organization, City Relief is connected to hundreds of faith communities whose sacred text says that we're supposed to help the poor and the marginalized, not *just* pray for them. The foundational text for the organization can be found in the book of Isaiah, chapter 58:6-7 (NLT), " . . . this is the kind of fasting I want: free those who are wrongly imprisoned; lighten the burden of those who work for you. Let the oppressed go free, and remove the chains that bind people. Share your food with the hungry and give shelter to the homeless. Give clothes to those who need them, and do not hide from relatives who need your help."

Over the years, I trained and mobilized thousands of volunteers as they showed up to engage the homeless community in New York City and New Jersey with a variety of motivations. But there's clearly a universal human need for significance that transcends culture, religion, socioeconomic status, and ethnicity. There are so many people out there who care and want to make a difference but often don't know where to start. I have watched thousands of people generously begin to volunteer their time without knowing anything about the people we serve or understanding why they can't maintain a stable living situation. These volunteers often arrive unsure, but leave fulfilled, and continue to come back because they find out that giving *of* yourself is always more meaningful than spending *on* yourself.

So the beauty of bringing people from all walks of life together to serve and care for those experiencing homelessness is that it positively impacts everyone involved in some way. But the problem is this: Most of us have no clue what to expect when we cross the cultural divides of socioeconomic status, religion, culture, or race, and that cluelessness makes us uncomfortable. Too often, we do away with the discomfort by creating narratives about the people we encounter who are different from us. When we see that tent pop up under the freeway and notice a grizzled man sitting beside it smoking a cigarette, we often subconsciously make up a story about who he is and why he's there. We base it on news reports, things we have heard from friends and family members, or maybe even on a single interaction we had with somebody else at a grocery store or a gas station who resembled him.

Or maybe it happens when we are walking through a subway station to get to an appointment and see someone sprawled out on the ground. Instead of asking him how he got there, most of us will mentally fill in the gaps. We give ourselves another reason not to have to speak to him. We already know what he would say, and why he is living the way he does. Before we can even process what we're thinking and why we're thinking it, we've walked by him and gone on our way.

We must take the time to critically examine some of the lies about our homeless neighbors that too many of us accept and pass on to others without even realizing it. I know that I started working with people experiencing homelessness with very little understanding of how and why someone might end up sleeping in a shelter or on the street. Even as someone who came very close to being evicted on a number of occasions myself, I was never *really* on the brink of being unhoused. I could always fall back on the generosity of my family and my friends.

There was a period when my wife and I were in between homes and we needed to board our dogs and live out of our car for a few weeks. It was short term, and definitely stressful, but we had friends reaching out almost daily to make sure we had everything we needed, and as a result, we always managed to find a house or a church that would let us crash indoors. As middle-class white people from the suburbs with access to technology and community networks, we had a predisposition for economic stability.

I once heard someone say, "One of the privileges of being privileged is not being forced to recognize that you are privileged." I honestly never thought about all the ways that I could avoid being homeless until I had to help someone else escape it for themselves. I made so many assumptions about so many people, and when I was finally confronted with my own ignorance, I wasn't ready to accept it until I was close enough to touch it.

INTRODUCTION

In part one of this book, I will attempt to dismantle four of the most commonly held stereotypes about our neighbors with no doors: that they are lazy, dangerous, mentally ill, and addicted to drugs or alcohol. The harm we cause when we hold these beliefs, or fail to correct them when expressed by others, is hard to overestimate. And they certainly get in the way of effective outreach to unhoused people. I will also explain how and why to interpret information and stories about people living on the street so that you do not reinforce these mistaken beliefs in yourself or others.

Part two is full of practical, actionable tips on how to engage with and effectively advocate for the unhoused people around you. I will begin with how to respectfully and helpfully make contact with homeless people you encounter on a regular basis. Then I'll explain how even someone with very little expertise can help connect those people to specialized, often life-changing services. And finally, I will dive into how you can begin creating real community with the unhoused people in your life, avoiding potential pitfalls and intentionally building spaces for connection across socioeconomic differences.

Finally, I will end with several stories of my homeless friends accompanied by photographic portraits they generously agreed to have done for this book. I chose to finish the book this way because the purpose of this project — indeed, of all my work — is to respect the humanity of our neighbors. It's my hope that by the end, you will be educated and inspired to join me in this mission.

Part One:
The Lies We Tell about Homelessness

Lies about Laziness

The doorbell rang at the City Relief base of operations in Elizabeth. We had just returned from a day of outreach and the staff members were sitting around doing paperwork. I opened the door to a gentleman standing outside with some papers in his hands. He was in his mid-40s. About five feet nine inches tall, he was a handsome man with a small mustache and sad eyes.

"Can I help you?" I asked.

"Yeah, uh, I need some help."

Having people ring our doorbell and ask for help is not an uncommon occurrence, but since we primarily do outreach and care coordination through our popup outreach events around New Jersey and New York City, we don't have an intake process for helping walk-ins

"My name is Josiah. What's your name?"

"Brian."

"Nice to meet you, Brian. I'm really sorry, my man, but right now we aren't in a position to do much for you. We just got back from outreach, where we gave away all of our supplies and honestly, most places that we could refer you to are closed this late in the day. Out of curiosity, how did you find us?"

Brian explained that he met one of our outreach leaders at one of our weekly pop-up events in Newark the week before.

He had recently been released from jail and was trying to rebuild his life. He was placed in a shelter in Newark when he was released but he no longer felt like he could stay there. He confessed to me that he had struggled with heroin addiction for years and just when it felt like he was free, he got pulled back in.

"There are drugs everywhere at this shelter and if I want to keep moving forward I need a new place to stay." He told me he was willing to do whatever it takes to make progress.

"How did you get here today?" It occurred to me that if his shelter was where I thought it was, he must have gotten a ride.

"I walked."

"You walked?" I was shocked. "You walked from Newark Penn Station? You didn't catch the train or a cab? How long did that take you?"

"About two hours," he replied nonchalantly.

I invited Brian inside. Even though I didn't know if there were any viable alternatives for him, he had come so far already. I have never been desperate enough to walk two hours for the *possibility* of meeting someone who didn't even know I was coming. The determination it takes to risk going all that way for nothing is incredible.

I ended up working with Brian for several years. I bought him a bus ticket to a rehab program in Louisiana because he was desperate to definitively sever all ties with the drug dealers and friends in the tristate area. I promised that I would bring him home if it wasn't the right fit. A few months later he was back in my office, back on drugs, and living out of an abandoned warehouse. I got him and one of his friends into a detox center in Manhattan which led to him getting into a 90-day, inpatient rehab program upstate. A year later I met him at his apartment in western New Jersey where he was living clean and sober near his new full-time job. Brian's journey has been anything but smooth sailing. But in spite of everything, he continues to work. He continues to show up. He continues to fight. But, more importantly, he had already worked harder than I ever will long before he got clean.

The lie that homeless people are lazy persists largely unchecked. I have met lots of individuals over the years who cling to the idea that they're housed and stable *because* they work hard, and that those who are unhoused and unstable must not. But I have worked with people living on the street like Brian for a long time now, and I can tell you unequivocally: that is complete nonsense.

First, it may surprise you to learn that many people who experience homelessness are already employed. One survey done by the Institute for Children, Poverty & Homelessness found that 31 percent of homeless parents had paid positions, with 65 percent of those working full time.[1] The problem is that employment doesn't guarantee housing. The minimum wage in America right now is $7.25 per hour. The national median price for a one-bedroom rental home in 2020 was $1,017 per month.[2] That means that the average person making minimum wage would have to work 140 hours per month, or 35 hours

---

1 Institute for Children, Poverty & Homelessness, *The High Stakes of Low Wages: Employment among New York City's Homeless Parents* (May 1, 2013), https://www.icphusa.org/reports/3884/.

2 Andrew Aurand et al., National Low Income Housing Coalition, *Out of Reach* (2020), 2, https://nlihc.org/resource/nlihc-releases-out-reach-2020.

per week, to afford such a rental, but that wouldn't leave them with a penny leftover for food, clothing, phone bills, transportation, or anything else.

According to the National Low Income Housing Coalition, the average minimum wage employee would need to work 97 hours per week to afford a fair market rate two-bedroom apartment. The NLIHC defines housing that's "affordable" as anything that costs less than 30 percent of one's monthly income. In 2020, the NLIHC put the national housing wage, or the amount someone would have to make to afford a fair market two-bedroom rental without spending more than 30 percent of his or her income, at $23.96 per hour.[3]

Consider Saheed Adebayo Aare. The publication *The City* featured his story in an article in February 2021:[4]

> A little after 5 p.m. six days a week, Saheed Adebayo Aare begins the odyssey to work, rolling his wheelchair down a ramp at a men's shelter on Wards Island.
>
> The 31-mile one-way trek takes him from a bus to two subway lines, needing six elevators, then onto another bus and finally rolling his

---

3 Alicia Adamczyk, "Minimum wage workers cannot afford rent in any U.S. state," Make It, July 14, 2020, https://www.cnbc.com/2020/07/14/minimum-wage-workers-cannot-afford-rent-in-any-us-state.html.

4 Jose Martinez, "From Wards Island to Amazon Warehouse in Jersey, This Commute Is Hell on Wheels," *The City*, February 28, 2021, Life, https://www.thecity.nyc/life/2021/2/28/22305812/amazon-warehouse-nyc-commute-by-wheelchair.

wheelchair two miles through Carteret, N.J., to his seasonal job at an Amazon warehouse. Aare, a 26-year-old athlete, spends more time on his round-trip commute—six or seven hours, usually—than he does at work, where he sorts orders for the online giant from 8:15 p.m. to 12:15 a.m., six days a week. In other words: He commutes about 40 hours a week so he can work 24 hours at an hourly wage of $15.25.

In large part due to this article, Aare got a transfer to an Amazon warehouse much closer to his shelter.[5] His commuting in a world that isn't built for people with his disability makes his perseverance particularly impressive. But the fact that he's both homeless and employed is not remarkable. Thousands of homeless Americans are working constantly but still don't make enough money to pay for a roof over their heads.

Sam spent more than 10 years on the streets. He left home when his mom made it clear he was no longer welcome in her apartment. They had a rocky relationship for years. She blamed him for his father leaving and showed preferential treatment to his sister. They fought constantly. She was livid that he decided to pursue his education instead of "providing for his family" by finding a low wage job. He was almost finished with his bachelor's degree in criminal justice at the time, but buying books and getting to class became impossible when he lost the ability

---

5 Jose Martinez, "Man's Amazing Journey to Amazon Made Smoother Thanks to Public and Private Help," *The City*, March 21, 2021, Work, https://www.thecity.nyc/work/2021/3/21/22343131/amazon-worker-gets-bronx-job-homeless-commute.

to sleep indoors. Surviving when you have no network and no support system is more than a full-time job. Meeting basic needs takes an inordinate degree of energy, let alone studying for tests and writing papers.

After dropping out and surviving in the streets and subways for over a decade, Sam accepted an internship with City Relief that provided stable housing for a year and a stipend to cover living expenses. He served in the streets with our team on a daily basis and was able to finally complete his criminal justice degree. But unfortunately soon after he graduated the internship program, our funding disappeared and there were no transitional housing options for him. He ended up right back on the streets. Even with a bachelor's degree, Sam struggles to make progress, because you need a home to get a job, and you need a job to get a home. The gravitational pull of homelessness requires anyone fighting against it to work twice as hard to get half as far. Sam keeps fighting and has been working as a night shift security guard for more than three years. In spite of all the obstacles in front of him, he pushes forward one step at a time. Sam is one of the hardest workers I know.

But what about homeless folks who aren't employed? Well, the truth is that it takes a tremendous amount of *work* just to survive with nowhere to sleep. Like Sam, trying to stay in school without a roof over his head, anyone trying to hold down a job without a place to rest, store personal belongings, and shower is going to have a difficult time. We often stereotype people we don't understand, and because many of us almost exclusively experience homeless folk as panhandlers on the sidewalk, many of us assume that *all* homeless people are "begging" for money instead of "working" for a living.

The idea that panhandlers aren't working hard is false. I have never tried to panhandle but I did work in sales for a number of years for a kitchen remodeling company. People who wanted new kitchen countertops or cabinets would reach out to our company for a free estimate and I would go to their homes, walk them through their options, and try to persuade them to give me a check. It was not an easy job. I did not always like driving from place to place, ringing the doorbell of some stranger, and then lugging samples of granite and cabinet doors into a different house and acting like their kitchen was the most important thing in the world to me. But I did it, because if I failed, my wife and I wouldn't make rent.

At no point in my sales role did I ever have to make cold calls or approach people as they were on their way to do something else. Everyone I gave estimates to were at the very least interested in a new kitchen. I had it so easy! I never had to step into someone else's personal space and hope that they didn't knock me out (except the time a woman bought a countertop from me against the wishes of her husband —he came pretty close). At no time was my personal financial desperation completely obvious to the customer.

There are clear differences between sales and panhandling. All I am saying is that neither is for the faint of heart. It's hard work to humble yourself and ask for anything. And even the *minority* of panhandlers who might be hustling decent money from compassionate strangers are doing so strategically and with a measure of determination and effort that should be admired and not maligned. This became abundantly clear to me when Covid-19 hit New York City in March of 2020. When all the tourists and wealthy pedestrians evacuated the city, only the essential service providers and unhoused people remained outside. Seemingly overnight our lines at City Relief doubled because the people who normally paid for their food by panhandling had to come to us. I spoke to countless individuals who expressed frustration because they couldn't provide for themselves doing the one thing they felt equipped to do.

Moreover, almost every job out there requires a certain amount of income and resources just to get started. A few years back, my wife and I were walking through Lower Manhattan one Sunday morning when we met a gentleman who was sitting on the sidewalk surrounded by bags. He was middle-aged with a beard and rough hands. He looked like he could have been taking his lunch break from a construction job. I struck up a conversation with him and found out he was homeless. He was also a certified electrician who received a job offer that he could start right away if he could *only* supply his own hard hat and work boots.

This man had skills, training, and even a job offer. He was a homeless man who got a job. He just couldn't *do* the job because he didn't have the income and the resources to show up and *start* the job. If it's not a hard hat and work boots, it might be a suit or a cellphone. Maybe slip-proof shoes, if someone is trying to work in the restaurant industry. One will also almost certainly need transportation to and from work, and not many jobs provide money up front for car or bus fare. How are you supposed to get a job if you can't get *to* the job? Plus, there's the simple fact that on every job application I've ever seen, directly beneath the line asking for your name, there's one asking for your address.

Besides panhandling, another thing we often mistake for laziness is hopelessness. How many times does one have to feel the sting of rejection before giving up altogether? And that rejection doesn't just come from potential employers. Many of the services that exist to help the homeless community are over capacity and under resourced. They consistently have to turn people away at the door. One term that politicians and news reporters use to describe homeless individuals who choose not to engage in treatment options or enter emergency shelters is "service resistant." This description makes it seem like these individuals don't want help. But one requirement for someone to accept help is the belief that help is actually available.

In New York City there are programs and opportunities for people struggling with homelessness to find work and get ahead, but they don't always provide the types of services that they advertise. At least not right away. There are often requirements and red tape that make their services what you might call people resistant. And in my experience, if a program is actually effective, it will be in high demand and hard to access. I met a man in Harlem once who told me that he was waiting on a city contracted outreach team to "spot" him so they could document his homelessness and get him a bed. The problem was that they needed to "spot" him three times over the course of nine months and they were not always where they said they would be. In frustration he shared about how he waited outside in a winter storm to get connected to their team, but they never came.

"I stood out there in the freezing cold all f*cking night!" He shouted. "They never came by and now I've been waiting for three weeks to be spotted again! I'm done!" I sometimes think it's a miracle that anyone makes it off the street.

Besides all these difficulties, there are other significant hurdles that people experiencing homelessness have to jump to land a job. For instance, you would be amazed at the number of people I've met over the years who don't have a state-issued photo ID or Social Security card. I've spoken to hundreds of people who lost everything when their bags or wallets were stolen while they were sleeping. I keep my driver's license on me at all times, but my passport, birth certificate, and other documents are in a fireproof safe inside my home. So even if I lost my wallet, it would be a minor inconvenience, not the catastrophe it is for so many.

I have a British friend named Ritchie, an actor who started volunteering with our organization about five years ago. I first met him in the South Bronx on an oddly warm day toward the end of December. I know it was warm, because while we were giving away coats to people on the street, Ritchie was taking layers off. Through the normal course of the outreach, I met a woman who was homeless and cold. Having slept outside for a few consecutive nights, her body temperature hadn't adjusted to the warmer weather that day and she was still shivering. She wanted to get off the street. I connected her to a private women's shelter in Lower Manhattan and arranged for one of my colleagues to drive her down there.

While I was speaking with her, I noticed that her coat was disheveled and dirty. I offered her one of the coats that I thought we brought with us to give away. She gladly accepted it. About 30 minutes after she left, Ritchie approached me and asked if I had given away his coat to one of our guests.

"I don't think so. Where was it? What did it look like?"

"It was on the pile of volunteers' coats in the outreach office and it was black. I saw a woman you were helping walk off earlier and I remember thinking how strange it was that she and I had the same coat."

"Pile of volunteers' coats? Those are not volunteers' coats; those are giveaway coats for our guests!"

It turned out that his coat also had his wallet and his apartment keys in the pockets. He was supposed to fly to London the following Monday and he was definitely going to need his green card and his driver's license to get on that flight. He asked me if he should be worried and I didn't have the heart to tell him the truth. I quickly pulled out my phone and called the staff member who had driven the woman downtown. She had just dropped the woman off and was on her way to pick someone else up. I called the shelter next.

"Hi, this is Josiah with City Relief. One of my colleagues just dropped off a woman to stay at your program tonight. I accidentally gave her one of my volunteer's coats with his ID, wallet, and apartment keys in the pocket. Is there any chance she is still there?"

"No, I'm sorry. As soon as your staff member dropped her off, she left. Let me go look outside to see if she is still around." My heart sank.

As I waited for the news that I believed would be bad, I looked into Ritchie's face and felt terrible. I assumed the woman I sent to the shelter must have noticed what was in the pocket of her new coat while she was being transported and decided the wallet was worth more than a night or two on a bunk bed in a dorm room. The shelter staff member came back on the phone.

"Nope. I'm sorry. She's gone."

"Okay. Well, if she comes back, could you please ask her if you can have the wallet and the keys? She can keep the coat." I turned to Ritchie and relayed the news. With a resolute sadness and a calm but exasperated tone, he replied, "I am going to have to stomp around a little bit." I nodded understandingly.

Ritchie was flying to England the following Monday. He was going to have to contact his credit card company, go home and get his passport, go to the DMV, replace his driver's license, and then work on replacing his green card, all before his flight. It was understandably frustrating. I probably would have done more than just stomp around.

But an hour later, I got a call from the chief operating officer of the shelter to tell me that, sure enough, the woman had made it back and she still had the wallet, the keys, and the credit cards. It was truly a miracle.

Try to imagine if Ritchie had kept every piece of identification that he owned in that wallet and it never came back. What could he have done if he had no passport? No mail with his name and address on it? No insurance cards? No birth certificate? The problem that many of our homeless friends have is that they are forced to carry everything they own on their person. If and when something gets stolen, misplaced, or damaged (which is way more likely when you're sleeping on sidewalks, subways, and in shelters), you can't just walk into the DMV and request a replacement. Just like one needs a home to get a job and a job to get a home, one needs ID to get ID. It can take years to build back one's identification portfolio. And in the meantime, finding a new job that's "on the books" will be virtually impossible.

And this problem doesn't just apply to those who lose their wallets or ID. It also applies to those who don't have any ID in the first place because they aren't legal residents of the United States.

Conversations on the news and around dinner tables about the issue of immigration don't even come close to accurately describing the experience I've had with homeless men and women who are undocumented. To start, there are lots of people who genuinely think that if someone is in the United States "illegally" while experiencing homelessness, they should just "go home." I have many friends and family who share this point of view, but I can tell you that the people I've spoken to on the streets, who are homeless and undocumented, are so under-resourced that even if they wanted to leave the country, they often can't. And some real, legitimate fears of what can happen during the process of leaving the country deter many who might otherwise do it.

I met Gregory in East Harlem when I first started doing outreach. He was an immigrant from Ghana. He traveled to the U.S. legally. He won his work visa through the immigration lottery and lived with his cousin while he worked as a taxi driver. Eventually, his cousin decided he wasn't paying enough for his rent. Gregory was already paying more than he could afford. They started fighting all the time about money and eventually Gregory decided that sleeping on the subway would be preferable to a life of constant conflict. But Gregory's boss gave him the job because his cousin made the introduction. Out of spite, his cousin got him fired. Without an address or proof of employment, he lost his visa as well. Gregory was open to going back to Ghana. But he didn't want to go to the embassy because he was afraid of being arrested and ending up in prison with no support or hope of getting out. He felt like a fugitive. He even stopped playing soccer in the park with a group of immigrant friends after two of them disappeared one day and he never saw or heard from them again. He assumed they had been picked up by Immigration and Customs Enforcement.

Another obvious problem with the thought that homeless undocumented immigrants should "go home" is that so many of them are already home. The well-known Deferred Action for Childhood Arrivals (DACA) program only exists because hundreds of thousands of people entered the United States as children.[6] Many of them didn't even know that they were undocumented until later in life.[7] I spent most of my childhood in Yaoundé, Cameroon. I loved it there. Even so, if you told me today that I would have to permanently relocate back to Cameroon next week, after I've spent 20 years working to establish my family and livelihood in the United States, I would run and hide. This is my home.

There are rarely great job opportunities for people who are underemployed and who lack the financial resources to find them. There are even fewer for those who come to the United

---

[6] "What is DACA and Who Are the DREAMers?", Anti-Defamation League, September 11, 2017, Updated August 2021, Tools and Strategies, https://www.adl.org/education/resources/tools-and-strategies/table-talk/what-is-daca-and-who-are-the-dreamers.

[7] If you'd like to read an excellent book on the subject, check out: *Dear America: Notes of an Undocumented Citizen* by Jose Antonio Vargas.

States in search of the American dream but overstay their visa. For them, the only options for jobs are off the books. This is why so many people find work in parking lots where contractors can find day laborers for less than minimum wage.

Leroy was a well-built man from Jamaica who told me that he was recently released from prison and didn't have anywhere to stay. He did ten years behind bars for transporting drugs across state lines and was trying to restart his life. He was also an undocumented immigrant. I spoke with him for a little while about options, and we settled on a Christian program on the Lower East Side that would accept men regardless of their immigration status. I prayed with him and then put him on a train so that he could get there. Fast forward about a year, and I was back in the same location doing outreach when a really fit man in athletic gear approached one of my volunteers and asked for me by name. I looked up and saw that it was Leroy.

"Leroy! What is good, man? You look amazing!"

"Thank you!" he said. "I just wanted to come by and thank you for helping me. I graduated from the program that you sent me to, and I just ran the New York City Marathon last week!" He proudly showed me the medal he received for completing the race.

I was blown away. There's a running club for men and women experiencing homelessness called Back on My Feet. It's a national organization that combats homelessness through the power of running, community support, and essential employment and housing resources. It currently operates in 14 major cities across the United States. Leroy joined Back on My Feet while he was in the residential program and found a new lease on life. He was doing amazingly well. But he was still undocumented. And still out of work.

This man completed his entire residential program, and the New York City Marathon. Yet, because of his immigration status, he could only do occasional jobs that were off the books and that he heard about through word of mouth. Every job he found was short term and low paying. He was doing well and working hard, but his circumstances were holding him back.

The reality that we have to face head on is that homelessness is often *not* the result of individuals making bad decisions. It is instead the result of our collective failure to prioritize the needs of the most vulnerable. The most common rationalization for these priorities is money. Lawmakers often think it is a poor investment to spend millions of dollars on affordable housing and social service programs that exist for those who generate the least amount of wealth. But the cost of letting people slip through the cracks is enormous. There are price tags for everything from emergency room visits to drug and alcohol treatment to police intervention and court fees. According to the United States Interagency Council on Homelessness, the taxpayer cost for one chronically homeless individual can be anywhere from $30,000-$50,000 per year.[8] We are not saving money by refusing to invest in programs that help our unhoused neighbors. I believe with all my heart that each individual deserves a chance at a better life simply because they exist. But it also makes financial sense to stop the bleeding and

---

8 United States Interagency Council on Homelessness, *Ending Chronic Homelessness in 2017*, 2017, https://www.usich.gov/resources/uploads/asset_library/Ending_Chronic_Homelessness_in_2017.pdf.

pay now so we don't have to pay more later. Unfortunately, one very easy way to stop us from making these positive policy decisions is to lean on the stereotypes we have discussed in this chapter.

But it's a lie that all someone needs to make it in America is hard work. The sheer amount of effort that it takes to find, acquire, and maintain even a job that doesn't pay a living wage keeps thousands of the hardest working people out there on the margins of society. So let's put to rest the idea that unhoused folks are lazy. Most of them have worked harder than you can imagine. And for some, no amount of work is enough to get ahead.

Lies about Danger

It was a beautiful summer day when we parked our outreach vehicle right in front of the basketball courts at Chelsea Park on West 28th Street. We had lots of volunteers, and lots of guests were hanging out enjoying the music and the atmosphere. There was a group of five or six guys playing basketball on the other side of the fence where we set up. People were eating and laughing. Then everything changed.

A homeless man in his 40s or 50s came wandering down the street toward our outreach, instigating arguments with every step he took. He was tall and towered over everyone around him. He was bald and had strong arms. He carried a small black backpack that looked tiny strapped to his large shoulders. But as big as he was, you heard him before you saw him. He got in line for soup, and by the time he made it to the serving window, I had deescalated two or three separate altercations. He was cursing out and insulting everybody. He bullied and provoked anyone who got in his way. He got his soup and fruit punch and then he yelled at the top of his voice, "You think that Jesus provided this for you? F*ck Jesus!" He then spat on the ground and shoved another guest.

I approached him tentatively and said, "Look man, you don't have to be like that. Just take your soup and go somewhere else."

"F*ck you! I will do what I like. You are a false prophet!"

"Okay. Fine. Then why are you hanging around? Just leave." I was asking more than telling. There are times when being bold and confrontational is the right way to go. This wasn't one of those times.

The guys playing basketball stopped their game and were on the other side of the fence watching the whole thing play out. They were young and athletic, probably in their 20s, maybe younger. Several of them weren't wearing shirts, and had I not been distracted by the man directly in front of me, I would have definitely been intimidated by their washboard abs. One of the shirtless basketball players spoke up, "Why are you letting him talk like that?"

I was surprised to hear him direct his question at me. Why was *I* letting him talk like that? I wasn't. I was trying to get this guy away from our outreach before someone took him up on his offer to fight. I sensed the situation slipping away from me.

"He's just talking," I responded. "Let him talk."

"Someone needs to teach this guy some respect." The basketball player snapped. His reply wasn't encouraging.

"Come on, just go back to your game. He's leaving anyway," I said hopefully. I realized that this big guy with a mouth was going to be a problem that I might not be able to handle.

Unfortunately, the big, bald man heard the comments from the basketball player.

"Teach me some respect? Teach me some f*cking respect? Come teach me then!" He was glaring at the basketball players as he yelled. He wanted to fight someone from the moment he set foot on 28th Street, and he finally had a taker. He threw his tiny backpack on the ground and started pacing back and forth while he continued to talk trash to the basketball player 20 years his junior.

"Okay. I'm coming." The basketball player jumped up onto the ledge where the fence dropped low enough for someone to climb over, and he started to make his way closer. He moved like a cat. The big guy was a lost cause, but maybe I could convince the basketball player to go do some sit-ups or find some weights to lift. I maneuvered between them and approached him.

"Look, man. He's not worth it. He's just running his mouth. He's wanted to fight since he got here. Just go back to your game. Plus, my coworker just called the cops, so they should be here soon." I don't know if it was the threat of police involvement or if I was more persuasive than I felt, but he paused. His friends were calling him back too. They wanted to play basketball.

"All right, f*ck that guy." He jumped back down off the ledge and started to make his way back to the court.

The big bald loudmouth saw him walking away and yelled, "Hey motherf*cker, want some soup?" He hurled his almost full cup of hot soup at the basketball player. It was a fine toss. The soup rained down onto his bare back and head.

The basketball player winced briefly, but then he turned, and in two strides he had leaped the fence separating the basketball courts from the sidewalk and he was on top of the soup quarterback like a lineman roughing the passer. He punched him in the face again and again. I didn't even have time to pivot. But when I did, I saw the rest of the basketball players running over to join him.

I intercepted one guy before he could jump on the pile, but I couldn't do anything about the other five. And then it wasn't *just* the basketball players. As soon as the big man was on the ground, several of the men he provoked earlier decided to get their kicks in — literally. The guy I grabbed was smaller than me and not all that interested in fighting. He immediately relaxed in my grip.

"I'm cool. I'm cool."

It didn't matter. The big bald man just curled into a ball while everyone else punched and kicked him relentlessly. His head was bleeding. What felt like hours later, even though it was probably just a few seconds, some construction guys who were enjoying the show on their lunch break meandered into the fray and broke it up. I ran over to the guy on the ground to check on him.

I yelled, "The cops are on their way!" The basketball players ran off up the street. The big bald guy stumbled to his feet and tried to limp after them. Apparently, he had a death wish. One of our regular volunteers, a forty something guy named Mike, and I each took an arm and led the big bald guy in the opposite direction from the basketball players.

"They will kill you, man. Let it go." I was trying to talk some sense into him as we led him up the street. He resisted us at first but eventually allowed us to lead him away. When we got to the next block, he took his bag from Mike and started to cross the street. "Wait," I yelled after him. "Do you want me to call an ambulance? Your head is bleeding."

"No. I'm just going to the train."

LIES ABOUT DANGER

I just shook my head as I made my way back to the outreach. I saw my colleague waiting for me with his phone to his ear.

"The police want to know if we still want them to send someone to help us?"

"Nope," I replied with an exasperated smile. "Tell them we have it completely under control."

So why start with this story when I'm trying to debunk the lie that homeless people are dangerous? For too many, wouldn't it just confirm the stereotype? In reality, there are scary people everywhere — among every group of people — and I didn't give you any evidence that the big man's homelessness had anything to do with his aggression. Recently on Twitter, I saw a viral video of a guy punching two others at a Denver Nuggets basketball game. I also witnessed a brawl at a music festival as my wife and I were walking from the merchandise table to the concert venue. Yet few of us would consider all NBA or music fans to be "scary." Out of hundreds of people we served that day in Chelsea Park, one guy started the fight, and a handful of others, many of whom were not homeless, finished it.

Over the years I have spoken to thousands of people experiencing homelessness and the vast majority are peaceful, patient, and kind.

In fact, homelessness is much scarier than homeless *people*. Over the last 10 years, I have found that far more people living on the streets and in shelters are victims of crime than perpetrators. There *are* obviously people on the streets who can present danger. Tragic stories like the unhoused person who beat people to death in Chinatown in 2019,[9] or the subway stabbings perpetrated by a homeless individual in 2021 make this clear.[10] But even in extreme cases like that, we often fail to notice that the victims too were homeless. Many people without the safety or protection of their own private residence are vulnerable targets. I have also found that homeless folks are less likely to report violent crimes, even if they're the victims, because they may have had negative interactions with police and do not trust the criminal justice system.

Unhoused people are often forced by circumstance to reside in dangerous places because they don't have the financial resources to live anywhere else. When I walk through Penn Station in New York City, I often see people sleeping on the ground as thousands of others walk by and around them on their way from point A to point B. I used to wonder why someone would choose to sleep in the middle of one of the busiest train stations in the country instead of finding a dark stairwell or quiet overpass. But the truth is that there is some protection that comes with being so exposed. The sad truth is that random acts of violence are often committed against the homeless community while they sleep. If they are hidden or tucked away, there is greater danger, and a greater chance of the perpetrators

---

9 Edgar Sandoval et al., "In Chinatown, Rampage Against Sleeping Homeless Men Leaves 4 Dead," *New York Times*, October 5, 2019, New York, https://www.nytimes.com/2019/10/05/nyregion/homeless-men-killed-chinatown.html.

10 Ashley Southall, Edgar Sandoval and Christina Goldbaum, "Four Subway Stabbings and a Young Man's Downward Spiral," *New York Times*, February 24, 2021, New York, https://www.nytimes.com/2021/02/24/nyregion/rigoberto-lopez-nyc-subway-stabbings.html.

getting away. Here are just a few headlines from news stories over the years that highlight the vulnerability of homeless individuals:

- Homeless Man Dies After Being Set On Fire In Oakland – *San Francisco Chronicle*[11]
- Assailant Sought In Unprovoked Attack On Homeless Man Recorded On Surveillance Video In Twentynine Palms – *ABC News*[12]
- Violent Spree Against Homeless People In Subway Leaves 2 Dead – the *New York Times*[13]

One article from *the Guardian* revealed a "shocking level of violence and intimidation" that homeless people experience in England and Wales. Researchers speaking to people without a place to live found:

---

11 Michael Cabanatuan, "Homeless Man Dies after Being Set on Fire in Oakland," *San Francisco Chronicle*, March 9, 2021, Crime, https://www.sfchronicle.com/crime/article/Homeless-man-dies-after-being-set-on-fire-in-16012906.php.

12 ABC News, "Assailant sought in unprovoked attack on homeless man recorded on surveillance video in Twentynine Palms." August 21, 2020, https://abc7.com/homeless-surveillance-video-attack-twentynine-palms/6382079/.

13 Andy Newman, Edgar Sandoval and Téa Kvetenadze, "Violent Spree against Homeless People in Subway Leaves 2 Dead," *New York Times*, February 13, 2021, updated May 14, 2021, New York, https://www.nytimes.com/2021/02/13/nyregion/nyc-subway-killngs.html.

- More than one in three have been deliberately hit, kicked, or experienced some other form of violence while homeless.
- More than one in three have had things thrown at them.
- Almost one in 10 (9%) have been urinated on.
- More than one in 20 (7%) have been the victim of a sexual assault.
- Almost half (48%) have been intimidated or threatened with violence while homeless.
- Six in 10 (59%) have been verbally abused or harassed.[14]

By and large, there's no reason to assume that homeless people are more likely to be violent than those who are housed. People are people. Homeless folks are in perpetual danger and surviving day by day with little recourse beyond sleeping with one eye open. These are neighbors with no doors to protect them and no alarm system to alert them if someone tries to harm them.

Moreover, the stereotype that people experiencing homelessness are dangerous is partially rooted in systemic racism. For centuries, the false narrative of the "dangerous" Black man has infected the social conscience of American society. And the unhoused population is disproportionately Black. African Americans make up 58 percent of the homeless population in

---

14 Dawn Foster, "Crisis report reveals shocking dangers of being homeless," *The Guardian*, December 22, 2016, https://www.theguardian.com/housing-network/2016/dec/23/homeless-crisis-report-attack-violence-sleeping-rough.

the New York City shelter system,[15] but only 24 percent of the city's general population.[16] Nationwide, African Americans make up 40 percent of the homeless population[17] and only 13 percent of the general population.[18] There are also racial disparities that affect economic opportunity. Before the Covid-19 pandemic, former President Donald Trump touted the historically low unemployment rates for Black Americans, but it was still almost double that of whites.[19] So we have to ask ourselves how much of our fear of unhoused people is mixed up in our fear of Black people?

Many people further assume that unhoused folks are dangerous because they are likely to have a history with the criminal justice system. And a lot of people I've met over the years who live in the streets, shelters, and subways do in fact have

15 Coalition for the Homeless, *New York City Homelessness: The Basic Facts*, updated September 2017, https://www.coalitionforthehomeless.org/wp-content/uploads/2014/04/NYCHomelessnessFactSheet_7-2017_citations.pdf.

16 United States Census Bureau, QuickFacts, New York City, New York, https://www.census.gov/quickfacts/fact/table/newyorkcitynewyork/RHI225219#RHI225219.

17 U.S. Department of Housing and Urban Development, Press Release HUD No. 21-041, March 28, 2021, https://www.hud.gov/press/press_releases_media_advisories/hud_no_21_041#:~:text=Almost%204%20of%20every%2010,(27%25%20or%2061%2C591).

18 United States Census Bureau, QuickFacts, New York City, New York, https://www.census.gov/quickfacts/fact/table/US/RHI225219#RHI225219.

19 Ben Popken, Trump touts "stupendous" jobs report - but black unemployment still rose again, NBC News, June 5, 2020, https://www.nbcnews.com/business/economy/trump-touts-stupendous-jobs-report-black-unemployment-still-rose-again-n1225706.

criminal or arrest records. But the idea that this automatically makes them dangerous is still false.

For instance, many people spend months or even years behind bars not because they have been found guilty of a crime but because they can't pay for bail. The Prison Policy Initiative estimates that over 400,000 people are currently being detained pre-trial, and that the median cash bail amount for a felony charge is about $10,000.[20] And even if someone has actually been convicted of a crime, almost half of all criminal convictions are for non-violent offenses to do with drugs, property, or public disorder.[21] The chance that someone will commit a violent crime, even after having committed one already, decreases drastically with age; the likelihood of committing a violent crime peaks in a person's late teenage years.[22]

Another reason someone's criminal record doesn't indicate that they are more dangerous than others is that, unfortunately, we have a criminal justice system that disproportionately targets communities that are economically disadvantaged. Or as the founder of the Equal Justice Initiative and bestselling author Bryan Stevenson says, we have a system that "continues to treat people better if they are rich and guilty than if they are

20 Prison Policy Initiative, Pretrial Detention, https://www.prisonpolicy.org/research/pretrial_detention/#:~:text=Nearly%20half%20a%20million%20people,%22hold%22%20on%20their%20release.

21 The Sentencing Project, Fact Sheet: Prisons and People in Prison, Facts About Prisons and People in Prison, updated August 2017, https://www.sentencingproject.org/wp-content/uploads/2016/02/Facts-About-Prisons.pdf.

22 Dana Goldstein, "Too Old to Commit Crime?," *The Marshall Project*, March 20, 2015, https://www.themarshallproject.org/2015/03/20/too-old-to-commit-crime.

poor and innocent. A system that denies the poor the legal help they need, that makes wealth and status more important than culpability."[23]

Additionally, this system is also tainted by racism. According to the NAACP, in 2014 Black men made up 34 percent of the prison population in America while only representing 14 percent of the general population. They go on to say that while white folks and Black folks use drugs at similar rates, the imprisonment rate of African Americans for drug charges is almost six times that of whites.[24]

As a result, it's no surprise that many homeless folks have criminal records, but that says a lot more about our system of mass incarceration and the larger issue of systemic racism in our society than it does about the unique danger of any one individual. In fact, once someone is labeled a criminal, a much more appropriate response than fear would be a healthy dose of empathy. Bestselling author of *The New Jim Crow*, Michelle Alexander, explains:

> Today it is perfectly legal to discriminate against criminals in nearly all the ways that it was once legal to discriminate against African Americans. Once you're labeled a felon, the old forms of discrimination —— employment discrimination, housing discrimination, denial of the right to vote, denial of educational

---

23 Bryan Stevenson, *Just Mercy* (Penguin Random House 2014) 313.

24 NAACP, Criminal Justice Fact Sheet, accessed June 9, 2021, https://naacp.org/resources/criminal-justice-fact-sheet.

opportunity, denial of food stamps and other public benefits, and exclusion from jury service — are suddenly legal. As a criminal, you have scarcely more rights, and arguably less respect, than a black man living in Alabama at the height of Jim Crow. We have not ended racial caste in America; we have merely redesigned it.[25]

The importance of resisting the lie that people living on the streets are dangerous can't be overstated. Systemic and personal discrimination against homeless people creates this stereotype, and then, in a vicious cycle, the stereotype actually works to reinforce patterns of discrimination. It is common when someone notices a homeless person in the neighborhood, they assume that person is a danger to their family. This concerned citizen might start to talk about it with other people in the neighborhood. Groups of concerned citizens may believe they are victims of community decline. These folks often wield their influence like a hammer and start to pound the local institutions into submission by blowing out of proportion stories about crime or harassment that would fly under the radar if the perpetrator weren't homeless, poor, BIPOC, or all of the above. More police are committed to the area. More security guards start popping up. Local news reports the concerned citizens' narratives of the situation. Policies and rules around "quality of life" issues start to make their way through local legislatures,

---

25 Michelle Alexander, *The New Jim Crow* (The New Press, New York, 2010-2012) 2.

and before anyone realizes it, this "neighborhood decline" is all people can talk about. Those who are actually experiencing homelessness, financial crisis, and emotional turmoil become abundantly aware that they are not welcome. And the primary reason they aren't welcome is the inaccurate perception that they are dangerous.

The irony is that, usually, members and leaders of these community watch groups say that they believe more resources should be dedicated to helping unhoused individuals, so long as those resources are being offered somewhere else. They will say things like "This isn't the right place for them" or "We aren't equipped to help them." Or "This is a family-friendly neighborhood. We have kids that need to be protected," as though poverty makes a person untrustworthy around children.

This view is often labelled with the acronym NIMBY, which stands for "not in my backyard." I recently logged into a virtual community board meeting for residents in the Financial District of Manhattan. A small number of noisy NIMBY voices on the Upper West Side of Manhattan had complained about the placement of homeless men in a hotel in their neighborhood, which happened so the men could leave their congregate shelter, have their own rooms, and isolate during the dangerous early days of the Covid-19 pandemic in New York City.[26]

The plan was for these men to move into a hotel in the Financial District, and the pushback was as instantaneous as

---

26 Janaki Chadha, "De Blasio faces public scorn, internal dissent over homeless move," *Politico*, September 9, 2020, New York edition, https://www.politico.com/states/new-york/albany/story/2020/09/09/de-blasio-faces-public-scorn-internal-dissent-over-homeless-move-1316295.

it was predictable. One of the vocal contrarians was a woman representing a local university because of the "many" parents of the students who attended that school who were "concerned" that the increased presence of homeless men in their community would create a safety issue for their kids.

In a 2019 *New York Times* article, Bill Bedrossian of Covenant House California was quoted regarding deterrents that demonstrate a lack of empathy on the part of communities toward the homeless population:

> "It's the worst it's ever been, as far as the backlash," he said. Residents of a street in San Francisco recently installed boulders on the sidewalk to deter people from erecting tents and sleeping there. In Los Angeles, homeowners have installed prickly plants for the same purpose.[27]

Another NIMBY argument that gets a lot of traction is that shelters and low-income housing facilities will present, not a physical danger, but a financial one. People are often afraid that such housing services will decrease local property values and hurt local business. In reality, there isn't a lot of evidence out there supporting this theory. In a 2016 article in the *Washington Post*, Terrence McCoy writes, "On average, researchers have found supportive housing facilities servicing the homeless and

---

27 Thomas Fuller, Tim Arango and Louis Keene, "As Homelessness Surges in California, So Does a Backlash," *New York Times*, October 21, 2019, US, https://www.nytimes.com/2019/10/21/us/california-homeless-backlash.html.

LIES ABOUT DANGER

other vulnerable populations rarely lead to higher crime rates or a drop in property values—and sometimes even raise the latter if the shelter helps stabilize a distressed community."[28]

At City Relief, we serve up to 200 people on any given day. The fact of the matter is this: in over ten years of outreach, I can count on two hands the number of truly scary people I've met. But if you see homeless people, assume they're criminals, change laws to make sleeping outside or panhandling illegal, and call the police when you see them again, you have successfully transformed human beings down on their luck into a bogeyman and a criminal. I can't tell you how many homeless folks I have spoken with over the years who have been harassed and ticketed for simply surviving in public without any viable alternatives. The lie that homeless people are scary is used to justify these prejudicial laws and make it as hard as possible for those without homes to exist in the public square.[29] And don't forget that ticketing someone with no money almost inevitably means that they will eventually get a court summons or a warrant that will lead that person directly back to the beginning of the street-to-prison pipeline.

Lastly, people often consider homeless folks unnerving because they're simply different. They don't conform to societal

---

28 Terrence McCoy, "D.C. residents fret over shelter plan, citing crime and property values," *Washington Post*, February 27, 2016, https://www.washingtonpost.com/local/social-issues/dc-residents-fret-over-shelter-plan-citing-crime-and-property-values/2016/02/27/7be82f4c-d978-11e5-925f-1d10062cc82d_story.html.

29 Juan Pablo Garnham, "As Austin voters weigh camping ban proposition, Texas lawmakers consider bills to prohibit homeless encampments statewide," *Texas Tribune*, April 27, 2021, https://www.texastribune.org/2021/04/27/texas-homeless-camping-ban/.

norms, not because they don't want to, but because their circumstances make it impossible. When they're sleeping on the subway, snoring, scratching themselves, or smelling badly, many people hold their children's hands a little tighter or move to the other end of the train car. Of course, those unhoused people are doing what everyone else is able to do when we're at home, comfortably tucked into our beds at night. But these folks don't have the luxury of privacy.

Because we don't know who that woman on the subway is, why she's there, or what she's capable of, we get scared. The only difference between that person and everyone else on the train is that she doesn't fit in. There could very well be someone we actually should fear on the same train who we wouldn't give a second thought simply because they blend in and our homeless neighbors can't. We need to stop living in fear of the unknown and learn about the struggles and challenges that our homeless neighbors face every single day. By accepting the lie that homeless people are dangerous, we only demonize a vulnerable population and perpetuate stereotypes that do real damage to our neighbors.

Lies about Mental Health

I met an older gentleman named James while doing outreach at the Port Authority bus station in Manhattan. He was holding a huge ceramic coffee mug. He would get soup and hot chocolate from our outreach vehicle and then find a seat on one of the chairs we set up on the sidewalk for our guests. He would pour his hot chocolate from the disposable paper cup into his ceramic mug before taking a sip. He always walked with determination, almost as if he were in a hurry.

James introduced himself differently depending on the day and who was speaking to him. Over several weeks, I learned that he believed he was part of a conspiracy to break a well-known celebrity arrested for child pornography out of jail so that he and the celebrity could move to Hawaii and be together forever. But FBI agents were trying to sabotage his every move. That's why he slept in an abandoned warehouse and had no ID or income. He was off the grid on purpose. He also believed that I worked for the FBI and was his inside man reporting directly to J. Edgar Hoover.

James would try to talk to me urgently every time I saw him. When he got my attention and we were talking one-on-one, he would ask in a hushed voice, "When are we going to Hawaii? I still need to get things in order. But I'll be ready by this weekend."

"Do you have an ID? You're going to need an ID," I would remind him. I sometimes tried to connect his beliefs to practical objectives. I'm not sure if that was the right thing to do or not, but my experience taught me that giving him undiluted truth didn't work.

"No. Can't your friends at the FBI get me the right ID?" He was certainly clever.

"I don't think so. We need this to be under the radar. Do you have your benefits card? A birth certificate?"

Some of my colleagues really didn't think I should encourage the delusion. In the beginning, I tried to persuade him that I wasn't actually an undercover agent, but it just didn't stick. His beliefs were the lens through which he saw the world. They weren't just factual errors that needed correction. They were experiential. They were tactile. I couldn't convince him that I wasn't an FBI agent any more than you could convince me that my two children are imaginary. I was there when they were born. I remember the way they felt in my arms. I hear them calling for me at home. When I think about them, I experience them. I see them. James experienced and saw things that weren't real. But they were real to him.

I've put lots of time and effort like this into serving many people with similar experiences to James. But I think for the average person hearing this story, it would be easy to conclude, as the media so often does, that a guy like James is a typical case among unhoused people, instead of an outlier.

It's true that more people suffering from chronic homelessness struggle with severe mental illness than the general public. One study in 2010 by the Substance Abuse and Mental Health Services Administration estimated that 30 percent of those experiencing homelessness for more than six months had mental illness with severe symptoms.[30] But 30% is not a majority, and many people are homeless for less than six months. The mental illness numbers drop significantly as the duration of homelessness decreases.

Moreover, in 2019, 51.5 million American adults, or one out of five, experienced some form of mental illness.[31] According to one study, "46 percent of Americans will meet the criteria for a diagnosable mental health condition sometime in their life, and half of those people will develop conditions by the age of 14."[32] But out of the approximately 328 million people living in the United States, about 580,000 Americans were counted as homeless in January of 2020.[33] This means that the vast majority of people experiencing mental illness are not homeless. So, we cannot chalk up our collective failure to prevent hundreds of thousands of our family members, neighbors, and friends from living unhoused to mental illness and

---

30 Substance Abuse and Mental Health Services Administration, *Current Statistics on the Prevalence and Characteristics of People Experiencing Homelessness in the United States* (last updated July 2011), 4, https://www.samhsa.gov/sites/default/files/programs_campaigns/homelessness_programs_resources/hrc-factsheet-current-statistics-prevalence-characteristics-homelessness.pdf.

31 National Alliance on Mental Health, *Mental Health by the Numbers* (last updated February 2022), https://www.nami.org/mhstats.

32 Ronald C. Kessler et al., "Lifetime prevalence and age-of-onset distributions of DSM-IV disorders in the National Comorbidity Survey Replication," *Archives of General Psychiatry* 62, no. 6 (June 2005): 593–602, https://doi.org 10.1001/archpsyc.62.6.593.

33 National Alliance to End Homelessness, State of Homelessness: 2021 Edition, https://endhomelessness.org/homelessness-in-america/homelessness-statistics/state-of-homelessness-2021/.

call it a day. Most of us have been impacted by mental illness either directly or indirectly. I know that mental illness is just a few branches up on my own family tree.

It's also true that, like James, some people are homeless specifically because their mental health symptoms led them there. But in my experience, homelessness is just as likely to cause or exacerbate mental illness as mental illness is to cause or exacerbate homelessness. Surviving day in and day out without a home is always a challenge to anyone's ability to differentiate useful coping mechanisms from destructive patterns of behavior. And as I will discuss, access to quality mental health care can be quite difficult.

It's not uncommon for us to generalize experiences we hear in a single story to an entire population. I watched the Will Smith movie *Concussion* and mistakenly walked away thinking that every ex-NFL player must have chronic traumatic encephalopathy (CTE) from all the head injuries and constant impact on the field. The assumption that all homeless people are mentally ill is about as accurate as saying that all NFL football players have CTE. While there's almost certainly a correlation, and even causation in specific instances, thinking all NFL players have CTE wouldn't be accurate.

Unhoused people experience life on the streets or in shelters, struggling every day to survive, not knowing if society cares, and constantly processing the stress of being unsure where their next meal is going to come from or whether their life will ever improve. It's the emotional and psychological equivalent of hiking a football and then slamming your head into a 300-pound defensive lineman over and over again. It isn't good for you, but that doesn't make mental illness the norm.

Furthermore, the stereotype of the mentally ill homeless person and the lie that homeless people are lazy mutually reinforce each other. As a society, we tend to blame the people who suffer from mental illness for not pulling themselves together, instead of recognizing that they have a physiological or psychological condition beyond their control. We're much more inclined to thoughtfully seek solutions when someone has problems that we can see, measure, and easily understand. Mental illness is still widely misunderstood. This ignorance inevitably leads to impatience. You never know how symptoms of a cognitive or intellectual disability might be affecting someone. And some people who have symptoms like James are certainly not self-destructive. They didn't decide one day that living outside is just more fun. But if we fail to understand the mental and psychological dimensions of being unhoused, many people will throw up their hands and fall back on an assumption of laziness.

All that said, it is true that, while mental illness is not typical for unhoused people, they do live with mental health conditions somewhat more frequently than housed people. And if we are to understand our neighbors with no doors, we need to destigmatize mental health conditions. The first step in destigmatizing anything is to learn about it.

There is a huge range of severity and symptoms in mental health conditions. And right now, mental illness is something many of us are grappling with whether we know it or not. As I write this, the United States is trudging through a global pandemic recovery and an economic crisis. As a result of forced isolation due to quarantines, long stretches of virtual learning for students, and thousands of businesses closing their doors, a lot of people are understandably having a hard time staying emotionally and mentally well. The Centers for Disease Control and Prevention reported in late June of 2020 that 40 percent of American adults reported struggling with mental health or substance use.[34]

James was suffering from delusional beliefs. The chemistry and biology between his ears skewed his reality. Everything we see, feel, taste, hear, and touch is processed in our brains. Right now, as you read these words, your eyes are looking at the letters and your brain is giving them meaning. Then you're interpreting that meaning through the filter of your experiences and education. Imagine that one piece of that process was interrupted or broken. What would you do if the letters got scrambled? What if you interpreted them incorrectly? Or you grew up in a different culture and the meaning of these words didn't correlate to anything that you learned along the way? Our very ability to interpret reality hangs on our brain's ability to function in quite specific ways.

It's true that my friend James believed that I worked for the FBI. And it's true that he believed that we were scheming to break a celebrity out of jail so that he could run off to Hawaii. But that's not because he was unintelligent. And it's not because he chose to disregard logic and experience for the sake of his delusions. His brain was literally interpreting the data

---

34 Mark É. Czeisler et al., "Mental Health, Substance Abuse, and Suicidal Ideation during the COVID-19 Pandemic—United States, June 24–30, 2020," *Morbidity and Mortality Weekly Report* 69 (August 14, 2020): 1049–57, https://www.cdc.gov/mmwr/volumes/69/wr/mm6932a1.htm.

incorrectly, and he was not going to process the information in a different way.

Trauma is one of the many reasons our brains can start interpreting data incorrectly and creating narratives that lead to delusion. All of our homeless neighbors with mental illnesses have experienced some form of significant trauma in their lives, because at a minimum, the experience of homelessness itself is significantly traumatic. But more likely, long before people find themselves living on the streets, they experienced abuse, neglect, or the deprivation of physical necessities like food, clothing, or shelter.

Some folks weren't born into circumstances that were traumatic, but they were born with a predisposition to physiological or psychological conditions. As a result of their genes, it may be impossible for them to thrive without the help of medications, therapy, or a support system. We need to stop stigmatizing them as "crazy" and recognize that they're dealing with a physiological illness that could just as easily impact us the same way. If we could provide low-barrier on-ramps for homeless individuals experiencing mental illness to get into supportive housing, or even the ever-scarce single unit with a private bathroom, as well as easy access to psychological and psychiatric assistance, we could minimize the number of people living on the streets tomorrow. Those of us with extra relational and financial resources can make a big difference by speaking up and supporting programs financially that already offer holistic treatment to men and women struggling with their mental health.

Simply getting access to a psychiatrist takes monumental effort, let alone getting access to treatment that's both helpful and dignifying. A rich person who has a psychiatric episode can spend thousands of dollars on a retreat center with 24-hour care, delicious food, art classes, and stunning scenery. But for homeless and low-income individuals, one of the only treatment options available to them is entering the psych unit of a hospital that's often under-resourced and overstretched. For others, getting help often means the risk of job loss and further disintegration of social support systems. The hard truth is that when we don't advocate for a robust public healthcare system, we end up allowing folks like James to unnecessarily fall through the cracks. The healthcare system is simply not set up to support people at the bottom of the economic ladder.

The last important point I'm going to make here is that the inaccuracy of stereotyping homeless people as mentally ill has significant consequences for the majority of homeless people who have no mental health conditions. A few years back, I did a workshop called "Understanding & Responding to our Homeless Neighbors," and one of the attendees was a woman named Sandra, who was experiencing homelessness herself.

As I spoke about the very real trauma and impact that mental illness can have on the healthiest and most educated people around us, she became visibly agitated. Sandra raised her hand during the Q&A portion and said, "I want people to realize that not all homeless people are on the street because of mental illness. Some of us just had bad luck. Some of us were victims of domestic violence and we left our homes in order to stay healthy." She was of course right, and there are real consequences for people like her when we make assumptions.

When politicians jockeying for power talk about how the primary solution to homelessness is supportive housing, it implies that every person struggling with homelessness requires round-the-clock treatment. And this takes energy and resources away from policies that would help the average homeless person — that is, those with no mental illness. I've spoken to so many people living on the streets who are frustrated because whenever they ask for help with housing or employment, they're forced to get a psychological evaluation. They feel like the implication is that everyone without a home must have some diagnosis that explains why they can't afford to pay rent. This can discourage them from seeking or consistently engaging in services. Just like with the belief that homeless people are dangerous, the assumption of mental illness among homeless people has consequences reaching far beyond simple, individual discrimination.

I have just barely begun what I hope is a longer journey for you of learning about the reality of mental health in the unhoused population. Knowing more on this subject will help you interact with a sizeable *minority* of people living on the street more empathetically and effectively. It will also improve your understanding of many people around you, whether or not they have a house. It will, in other words, make you a better neighbor to everyone.

Lies about Drug Use

Every year in New York City, there is a series of events called Don't Walk By. They are a collaborative experiment run by several faith-based organizations that exist to help people escape the perils of homelessness.

Every Saturday in February, hundreds of volunteers walk the streets of Manhattan looking for men and women with no place to sleep. Then the volunteers invite anyone who is interested to a church fellowship hall with food, emergency supplies, medical care, and direct service providers who can help them get off the street for a night or two and provide ongoing case management.

That last part is where I come in. One of my primary areas of expertise is navigating the bureaucracy of New York City social services. I had a colleague who reached out to me because he discovered that his daughter had relapsed into heroin addiction. She had just completed a short-term rehab program and was back at home. The parents helped her get a job at a local diner and all indications were that she was progressing nicely. But heroin addiction is rarely a one-and-done experience.

"Josiah, I don't know what to do. She has insurance through the state of New Jersey but since she was just in a program a few weeks ago, they likely won't take her back. Do you have any suggestions?" I thought about it and remembered there was a detox in the Bronx that would take people without insurance as long as they qualified as "homeless in New York City." I reached out to a friend who worked there and figured out the qualifications.

"Here's what you need to do: She is staying with you right? You will need to write her a letter of eviction. I know it sounds ridiculous, but she will need something on paper showing that she has nowhere to live. She will also need to be fired from her job, so that she can show that she is unemployed. Then we will have to drive her to the Bronx and drop her off in front of the detox, making her officially 'homeless in New York City.'"

That's sometimes what it takes to help someone get access to services that might save their life. The stakes are so high for people struggling with heroin or opioid addiction, and they are most vulnerable to overdose following a brief season of sobriety. This is why many people die soon after leaving jail or rehab.

During one Don't Walk By event, a volunteer approached me. "Josiah, can you help my new friend? She wants to get off the street." The volunteer led me to the table where she was sitting. She was eating her third plate of pasta. She had curly brown hair, and she was skinny. Really skinny. Her coat looked like it was three sizes too big and her hair was matted against her face. But other than appearing exhausted, she seemed in good spirits. She had managed to find her way indoors to a hot plate of food and a new pair of socks.

"This is Josiah," the volunteer said. "He helps people on the street connect with resources." The volunteer was already explaining the situation before I could say hello. The chair next to the woman with the extra-large coat was empty.

"Do you mind if I sit?" I decided to interrupt the well-meaning volunteer and start my conversation with this woman by asking for permission before sitting down next to her. Too many social service employees make assumptions about their clients that negatively affect their ability to build trust. Little things like getting an invitation to sit down next to someone can be the difference between them hearing you or not. It's all about autonomy. Homeless people are often told where to go, what to do, and how to go about it. People who want to help often assume that homeless people want their help and then everything just goes sideways.

"Of course." She gave me a big smile.

"Like this helpful person just said, my name is Josiah. What's yours?" Another helpful place to start when you're engaging someone who lives on the street is simply to introduce yourself.

"Becky," she replied. "It's nice to meet you."

"The pleasure is all mine, Becky. Tell me a little about your current situation." I always try to make it clear that I'm not interested in anything other than what someone is willing to share. I've been with many people when they're doing intakes into shelters and rehabs where they ask questions about someone's medical history, sexual history, criminal history, relational history, and religious history all within the first five minutes of learning their names. Less is often more.

"Well, I'm sleeping on the street and I'm a heroin addict," she said matter-of-factly. She then proceeded to lift up the sleeve of her massive coat and show me the track marks on her arms that were still trickling with blood. "I want to stop, but I can't go to the hospital."

"Oh yeah? Why not?" With heroin and homelessness, the hospital is often the first stop, because the withdrawal can be mentally and physically agonizing. "I could try to find a different option, but it would not be easy. Especially on a Saturday night."

"I've been kicked out of every emergency room in New York City."

I decided to test the theory. "Bellevue?"

"Yep."

"Beth Israel?"

"Yeah."

"Metropolitan?"

"Yes."

"Dang! You're not kidding!" There are more hospitals that I could have tried, but her unwillingness to give those a shot meant that connecting her with any services was going to be an uphill battle. "I don't suppose you have Medicaid, do you? A benefits card?"

"Nope. I got robbed on the train, and my Medicaid is restricted to Bellevue. I won't go there." I could hear the resignation in her voice. I wasn't sure that I'd be able to pull a rabbit out of the hat this time.

"So, your Medicaid is restricted, you don't have ID, you're shooting heroin, and you won't go to the hospital?" I was mostly just thinking out loud.

"I know. I don't think there's anyone out there who can help me."

"You're not making it easy for me, that's for sure." I said it with a smile on my face and she laughed with me. Making this kind of joke is risky in some situations, but humor can be relationally helpful when all someone knows is isolation and judgment.

"Would you be willing to try going cold turkey?" I knew it was a long shot. Cold turkey means just stopping outright. No medications, no tapering, no time to adjust. Just a long dark leap off the ledge of despair in the hopes of landing on your feet.

"Nope. I tried that and I ended up getting so sick, I thought I was going to die." She paused, then continued, "Look, I know I am a hard case. I told the person who found you that there was nothing you guys could do, but she insisted. I'm just grateful for the meal and the socks." She smiled again.

"I really wish you'd let me take you to a hospital. I'll walk you in. I'm much bigger than you are, so they will have a harder time kicking *me* out!"

Her smile this time meant that I was playing with the edge of her patience. You can't make someone do something they're unwilling to do. And if you try, your previously established credibility will be up for grabs. I was new at the time, but I wasn't a fool.

I folded. "Can we at least clean up your arms?"

"Absolutely." My wife, a registered nurse, was volunteering with us that night. I got her attention and introduced her to Becky. Within a few minutes they were best friends. My wife cleaned up the bleeding and put on some bandages. My wife told her about our lives while she worked, and Becky asked lots of questions about where we lived and what we liked to do in our spare time. She loved hearing about our beagles and shared about her own childhood pets that she had before her drug use spun out of control.

She stayed until the very end of the outreach. I tried to convince her to spend the night indoors at one of our programs. If I could go back in time, I would have strongly recommended that she get some medically assisted treatment (MAT). MAT is when someone who struggles with addiction gets prescribed medication like methadone, naltrexone, or buprenorphine to help minimize the cravings and protect from overdose. Unfortunately, there is still a lot of unnecessary stigma and skepticism around MAT in some circles, but in my experience with people living on the streets who are addicted to opioids like heroin, Vicodin, and Oxycodone, MAT saves lives. My interaction with Becky was 10 years ago, and I didn't know then what I know now.

She declined my offer for a night indoors because she didn't want to go into a congregate shelter environment. Once we had done everything we could, bandaged her wounds, and given her some emergency supplies, I walked her to the door of the church and realized that it was pouring rain outside. Most of the volunteers were collecting their umbrellas and running full speed to the subway platform a few blocks away.

"Do you want me to get you an umbrella?" Becky was going to get soaked.

"No, thank you." Then she turned back to look at me and gave me one more compassionate smile. "Thanks for everything. Get home safe, Josiah."

"You too." I choked on the last word. It's just what you say . . .

As Becky walked outside into the pouring rain and disappeared into the night, my heart broke. "Get home safe," meant so much more coming from her than any goodbye I had ever received. I would get home, sure. But my response to people stuck on the streets would never be the same. Becky is one of hundreds of people I have met over the years who struggle with homelessness and addiction. Stories like hers are unfortunately often generalized into lies about homeless folks and drug addiction, which, like the lies concerning mental illness, are used to dismiss their challenges.

There is a higher level of addiction among the homeless community than the general population, but it is still a minority. The federal government's Substance Abuse and Mental Health Services Administration published a report that estimates that in 2003, 38 percent of unhoused people were dependent on alcohol and 26 percent abused other kinds of drugs.[35] While the percentage of addiction understandably goes up the longer that someone stays homeless, most homeless people aren't addicted to drugs or alcohol.

For those who do use substances, we shouldn't take that fact as an excuse to minimize the responsibility we all have to help. Just like with mental health, empathy and education are the better path. So first, in many instances, just like with the housed population, drugs and alcohol are used as self-medication for both physical and emotional pain. This is often in place of the therapeutic and psychiatric services which are difficult for homeless people to access, as I explained in the last chapter. Living on the streets, under a bridge, in a tent on the sidewalk, or even in a shelter with dozens of strangers sleeping

---

35 National Coalition for the Homeless, *Substance Abuse and Homelessness* (July 2009), 1, https://www.nationalhomeless.org/factsheets/addiction.pdf.

in beds next to you is extremely stressful. Not having a job that pays a living wage, or feeling perpetually ignored and looked down upon can be soul crushing.

Beyond the emotional pain, there's the physical pain and sickness that many homeless people deal with as well. In a great article in *The Atlantic*, doctor and public health advocate Seiji Hayashi describes the connection between health and homelessness perfectly:

> Once homeless, the healthy become sick, the sick get sicker, and the downward spiral accelerates. In a study published in the Journal of the American Public Health Association, Monica Bharel and her colleagues found that homeless individuals used the emergency room almost four times more than other low-income residents of Boston. Bharel also calculated that approximately 6,500 homeless individuals cost the state's health care system $16 million a year in emergency room care, almost $2,500 per person. Managing chronic illnesses such as heart disease and diabetes is always challenging, but adhering to treatment regimens is nearly impossible while homeless.

I met my friend Even for the first time on a Sunday morning in February. There had been a Don't Walk By event the night before. After some convincing, Even accepted the invitation from some volunteers to spend the night indoors.

The next morning I led a City Relief team to the private shelter where the overnight guests stayed. We walked in at 6 am with breakfast, coffee, and gift cards to local fast food restaurants. I set up at a table in the back and offered to meet with each guest so that we could hopefully begin the process of getting them off the street.

Even was one of the last people I met with. I apologized for the wait.

"No problem at all. Your team is amazing! I had an incredible conversation with one young lady who is from Illinois, or was it Ohio? I can't remember. But she was so kind."

Even and I ended up speaking for about thirty minutes. I found out his full name was Even Michael Ross. He was sleeping in the street because he didn't feel safe in shelters. He was in his late 50s but 20 plus years in the streets had taken their toll. He had a high voice and a great sense of humor. When he was young he ended up on a documentary about the New York City drug scene. He insisted that I pull it up on YouTube and watch it when I got home. He started using heroin as a teenager but when I met him he was treating his addiction with methadone. We laughed and we cried. I instantly loved him.

That morning I referred him to several locations where he could start the process of applying for housing and access some additional services. He needed medical care for a leg wound that refused to heal because he rarely got a chance to sleep perpendicular to the ground. Gravity is never kind to feet and leg wounds when someone sleeps in the street.

I managed to stay connected with Even for a little while but eventually his phone broke and we lost touch. He wasn't making much progress and his leg wound got worse and worse.

Volunteers would sometimes report back to me after walking the streets with us that they bumped into someone in the street who needed bandages for his leg wound but who also wanted to get me the message that he loved me and was doing ok.

Eventually his leg wound got so bad he ended up at Bellevue Hospital. My teammate Teresa Gowan who is a social worker and an all-around rockstar connected with the hospital staff and advocated for them to perform surgery instead of just kicking Even back to the street. And we started working on getting him a placement in a rehab facility.

Unfortunately, his time at the rehab ran out and Even ended up back in the street. We tried to work with an organization that provides medical services for low-income New Yorkers, but there was a staffing change and Even's case was dropped in the transition.

Sometime later, I bumped into Even at a subway station in Manhattan and he gave me a big smile.

"Josiah! I've missed you! How have you been?" In the midst of everything, he was worried about me.

"I'm good, Even. How are you? Any progress with your case worker in finding you housing?"

"Not yet. My phone was stolen and I can't reach my case worker."

"Well, here is my card again. When you get another phone, call me and we will get you connected again." Once again, the fact that he didn't have a functional cell phone was blocking his ability to make progress. My train was pulling into the station and I had to be somewhere so I took a photo with Even to share with the volunteers who he had met over the years.

"Please call me as soon as you get a phone, my friend. It breaks my heart that you're still out here."

"I know. I will call. Don't worry!"

That was the last time I saw Even. Tragically, I found out a year later that he likely passed away. The average life expectancy for the homeless community is about 20 years less than the national average.

A few years later, I was interviewing a candidate for an outreach position with City Relief. I asked him about his most meaningful experience with someone in the street. He said, "A few years ago I met a man at Port Authority. He was the kindest man. He prayed for me and encouraged me so much. I will never forget him. His name was Even."

I was both encouraged and heartbroken at the same time. I had to tell this outreach candidate that the man who had encouraged him so much was now gone, in large part because our system failed him. He was too young for senior housing, too sick to survive in the streets, and too poor to pay for a room. I don't know what I would have done if I was in his shoes. I can't say for certain that I wouldn't turn to alcohol to stay warm while sleeping on the streets on a cold winter night, or turn to drugs to stay numb if I was dealing with physical and emotional trauma that limited my ability to make any quantifiable progress.

Becky and Even lived in the reality that for those living on the streets and struggling with addiction, getting help is never as simple as asking for it. Drugs and alcohol interact with each person's anatomy and physiology in different ways. The amount that someone uses, the duration of time that they've used on a regular basis, the medications they're taking for other health issues, as well as their access to health insurance, quality healthcare, and government-issued identification all impact how and where someone can go to get treatment. And while there are some amazing organizations out there providing free treatment options for people in financial distress, they are not always easy to find. Becky had Medicaid that was restricted to Bellevue Hospital. That means that her medical care would only be covered within that hospital or with a letter from that hospital affirming that the issues for which she needed treatment were legitimate and would be covered. Unfortunately for Becky, and hundreds of others I've tried to help on a Saturday or Sunday, the office that provides that letter is only open Monday through Friday.

Medicaid insurance can become even further restricted for a variety of reasons. Sometimes there's alleged fraud associated with the cardholder. This can happen because someone is transient and accumulates charges at different hospitals, causing abnormalities in the record that Medicaid finds suspicious. It also can happen because of the predatory practice of "Medicaid get paid" schemes. Sometimes in communities with high poverty rates, someone in the medical field will recruit people who have Medicaid to get some simple treatment like a teeth cleaning, stress test, or eye exam. Then the "office" that provides that service will overcharge the patient's insurance for some larger procedure and give the person 20 dollars for their trouble.

There was one guy who used to hang out at the City Relief Harlem outreach location who would walk around with a cup of our soup in one hand while he not so subtly said out loud, "Stress tests. Stress tests. Medicaid get paid." People would approach him and he would ask them for their benefits card.

After calling someone to confirm their Medicaid was in good standing he would bring the three or four "customers" over to a corner where a van was parked to drive them to the "clinic." Unfortunately, those who end up paying the price for these schemes are the ones who Medicaid marks as fraudsters, and all they wanted was a little cash to get through another day. There have been several times when I was trying to get someone who was finally ready to receive treatment into a detox program only to be told their Medicaid was "restricted." These predatory schemes can set people back right at the exact moment when they have a chance for real, positive change.

Becky also had a long and checkered history with the hospital where her coverage was restricted. I didn't know the details of her particular story, but hospital staff often become extremely jaded about treating repeat patients who use heroin. The staff sometimes prefer to get rid of those patients as quickly as possible, believing the patients' motivation for seeking treatment is just to get another medication prescription.

Another one of the biggest obstacles people have to overcome to get drug treatment is the simple belief that real change is impossible. People like Becky taught me that sometimes getting help is more about luck than it is about sheer force of will. I cannot count how many people I've transported to inpatient treatment over the years who were turned away because there was no bed available, or they needed to have their prescription medications before they could be admitted, or they didn't have the right insurance, or they weren't allowed to smoke cigarettes while going through treatment, or they didn't have anywhere to store their personal belongings. There are so many logistical barriers to tear down before people can even begin to wrestle with addiction.

Over the years, I started making efforts to prepare people for the worst possible experience imaginable while also trying to encourage them. Selling the benefits of sobriety without honestly disclosing the pain and stress of getting there almost never works out well for the person I'm trying to help, let alone for my credibility as an advocate. I now ask questions like "if I could get you into a program today but it would take hours and hours before you get a bed, would you still be interested?" Or sometimes, "Are you ready for the fight of your life?" When I started doing outreach, I thought it was my job to convince people struggling with substance use to get help. I would drive people to programs and drop them off without any transportation home because I was worried if I gave them an easy way out they would take it. I remember one guy we drove from the Bronx to Queens to get help only to find out that he walked all the way home instead of trying to get admitted. As a result, I started giving every person I sent to detox or rehab a MetroCard for a return trip just in case things didn't work out. I know other service providers and nonprofit staff who would discourage providing a "way out" for people who are considering entering treatment. There are even people out there who earnestly believe that jail is the best method for drug treatment because people inside don't have the option of running away. I disagree. As we already noted, one of the most dangerous times for people struggling with addiction is when they leave jail or rehab because their tolerance is lowered after being forced to cut back. Many of these folks were not choosing to quit because they wanted to, but because they had to. So when they finally have the option to use again, they might go back to the same quantities they were using before and can very easily overdose.

My questions may have discouraged some individuals from trying to change their lives, and providing transportation fare ahead of time can function as an escape hatch. But I am convinced that the risk of honestly preparing people for an uphill battle is worth taking. I'm not going to be dishonest with people, and the risk associated with that dishonesty is setting them up to fail, potentially causing significant trauma, overdosing, or even death. I understand why people use drugs or drink alcohol when they're living on the street. I might do the same. I also understand why they conclude that there is no point in trying to stop. It is only harmful to dismiss homeless people who use drugs. Instead, we need to remember that the gravitational pull of substance use is almost impossible for some to overcome without allies and advocates who will keep believing change is possible, even when there might be reasons not to. If you're trying to help people as effectively as possible, it's the only way.

So now I will turn to the practical steps you can take to become the sort of smart, confident advocate your neighbors need.

Part Two:

Becoming a Good Neighbor

Engaging Neighbors with Compassion

February in New Jersey can be pretty cold, but we don't always get much snow. In February 2021, we did — buckets of it. The combination of the worst winter in 10 years and the pandemic wasn't good for those with no place to call home. City Relief has always believed that one of the main ways we earn trust and credibility with people living on the street is to show up no matter what. But this philosophy isn't always easy to practice. On the occasional days that I wake up, look outside, and see snow drifting beautifully to the ground, it's extremely tempting to go back to bed.

On one such morning, the City Relief team agreed to drive into our base of operations to shovel the sidewalks and clean off the outreach vehicles. I got out of the house because I was determined to prove to the team that their fearless leader wasn't afraid to get his hands dirty and do some manual labor. I grabbed my shovel, cleaned off my car, and drove into Elizabeth. After shoveling for a couple hours, I headed home to get a jump on some remote office work.

As I was passing a 7-Eleven, I remembered that my wife asked me to stop and get some milk on my way home. I pulled into a snowbank that had until that morning been a parking lot. I managed to stop my car and get out. I remember thinking to myself, "I hope that I'm not stuck," as I walked quickly toward the entrance of the store.

I noticed a gentleman shivering beside a trash can near the doorway. He was older with bloodshot eyes. He was wearing a torn jacket that was way too thin for the frigid temperatures and the precipitation that had pounded our area for the previous week. I realized that he was probably hoping that customers would offer him change as they walked out of the store and back to their cars. I felt immediate compassion for him, but I was on a mission, so I made eye contact with him as I walked in and said, "I'll get you on my way out." As I walked into the store in search of the milk, I realized that I had a grand total of seven dollars in cash, a five and two ones.

I found the milk and decided to also get half and half while I was there. I knew I had a day of virtual meetings ahead of me, which would require coffee. I got the dairy products and I was trying to do the math in my head as I approached the register. I had to either pay with the cash and give the man outside what was left over, or pay with a credit card and be "generous."

The gentleman behind the plastic divider scanned my items and gave me the verdict: $6.70. If I paid with cash, it would leave a grand total of 30 cents for the man outside. I decided to pay with a credit card. As I walked out of the store, I made my way over to the man. I handed him the money and said, "You hanging in there?"

"Doing my best," he said.

"My name is Josiah. What's your name?"

My 10 years of working with homeless folks have taught me that asking for names are important, even if you don't get an answer. Showing an interest in someone's identity as a human being always goes a long way. But I've also learned that it's presumptuous to assume that a homeless person should give me their name before I offer my own. I have made that mistake many times, and just as many people have looked at me with confusion or suspicion as they said, "Why do you want to know my name?"

It's so common for us to assume that homeless folks should be happy — or at least willing — to share their personal information with us. It's not malicious, but it's ignorant. Homeless folks are often used to being treated with skepticism and judgment. Many are victimized and criticized by those of us with financial resources and houses. They're often treated as second-class citizens and looked at with disgust. They're also often picked on by police and local business owners who want them to "move along." It's very likely that someone in the not-so-recent past asked that guy panhandling outside of 7-Eleven his name so that they could report him for "vagrancy" or "loitering." But since I had learned the hard way, I introduced myself first.

"Marcus," he replied.

"Well, Marcus, I know it's not much. But I hope it helps a little bit. Please do your best to stay warm." I smiled at him and trudged through the snow back to my car. As I climbed into the driver's seat, I felt pretty good about myself. After all, I saw Marcus and I went out of my way to pay with a credit card so I could give him more than 30 cents. I even remembered to offer my name before I asked for his. I was on a roll. As I put my car in reverse and hit the gas, I quickly realized that the snowbank was deeper than I thought. The car rolled a little, and then halted. I shifted back into drive and tried to pull forward. Nothing.

Reverse. Drive. Reverse. Drive.

There was a driver behind me nervously watching me struggle. I'm sure they were concerned that at any moment I would find some traction and pull right into them. They had nothing to worry about. I was thoroughly stuck. After about five more minutes of pure futility, I put the car in park and started to unbuckle my seatbelt. As I opened my door, I heard a voice behind me.

"I got you. Get in and put it in drive." Marcus was jogging around behind my car to help. He enthusiastically pushed as hard as he could. I still couldn't get any momentum. Marcus saw my shovel in the back of my car and asked if he could use it.

"Absolutely! I will take whatever you can give me!"

Marcus shoveled around all four of my tires. Then he pushed some more as I tried to rock my car forward and backward. I started to move. Marcus pushed even harder while yelling out instructions. We worked for an arduous 30 minutes until Marcus managed to push me into the plowed street. I rolled down my window and yelled out to him, "You're my hero, Marcus!" And he was. I didn't want to sit there in that 7-Eleven parking lot for the rest of the day. As I started driving home, it occurred to me that I had patted myself on the back for giving Marcus five dollars just moments before he spent half an hour doing physical labor for me. I never said I always approach these encounters perfectly.

So let's talk on a very practical level about how you can approach similar interactions with unhoused people you meet, as well as how to think about those occasions.

ENGAGING NEIGHBORS WITH COMPASSION

We'll start with something that's simple, but important. Compassion always starts by seeing the person right in front of you. Fortunately for both of us (admittedly, more for me than him), I saw Marcus on my way into the store. If you want to do something about homelessness, you need to start by opening your eyes to the struggle of the people all around you. Who are the people in your community that need to be seen? Are they in the grocery store? Are they under the overpass? Are they in a tent community in the woods outside of your church? You will not engage with homeless people that you aren't trying to notice. We have been trained to walk by them. It takes serious intent to undo that programming.

Once you've started noticing the people around you, the next step is to engage with them. This is where a lot of people get tripped up. If you don't know what to do when you see someone in need, you will often end up doing nothing at all, even if you have good intentions. So the best things you can do are think through the dynamics of how you want to help, and plan ahead. I saw Marcus, acknowledged him on my way in to let him know I'd be back, planned my purchase in the store to have cash for him, and was ready to ask him his name and have a conversation.

Probably the single most common question I get about how to help from volunteers, donors, or even random people on social media is, "Should I or shouldn't I give money to unhoused people in my community?" Usually the concern behind the question is that giving money to someone could enable their addiction to drugs or alcohol. Of course, sometimes panhandlers do spend the money they raise on those things. But consider two things. First, as we've learned, most homeless folks do not struggle with addiction to substances at all. So most of the cash you hand out won't end up funding the purchase of a six pack.

Second, we need to reframe the issue of whether or not people will use the money we give them in a self-destructive or unhealthy way. Every two weeks or so, City Relief deposits money into my checking account. Nobody at the organization asks me how I use that money. The organization believes my contribution is worth the money that they pay me, so they don't ask. Let me get something off my chest. Sometimes I use that money to buy beer and ice cream. I know; it's not good for me. But those are choices I get to make because City Relief thinks there is value in paying me a salary. Similarly, if we think there is value in helping our homeless neighbors, we can give them that same freedom with their money.

Wherever you land after thinking through the dynamics of handing out cash, there are further issues to consider. If you do want to give money, make sure you have cash on you when you leave the house. Maybe set aside a certain amount each month to hand out so you don't have to think about what you can afford at the moment a request for money comes your way. Then, if the monthly money runs out, there are lots of tips to follow in the rest of this chapter.

One reason I don't always give money to people who are panhandling is that I don't like the relational dynamic it creates. My goal in almost every interaction with someone who lives on the streets is to connect with them as an equal. Tossing some money into a cup at someone's feet isn't usually the most effective way to send a message of equality. Ideally, if you are giving away money, try to introduce yourself and learn the person's name. Obviously be considerate of the person you're approaching — whether they seem to want to have a conversation, or whether you're stopping them from asking others for money. But in my experience, doing something is almost always better than doing nothing. Try not to settle for a transaction. I would have regretted not being able to thank Marcus by name if I hadn't asked him for it beforehand. And I'm glad I told him I would come back to talk to him when I was on my way into the store, instead of doing what I'm sure he was used to people doing and walking right by him.

If you don't want to or cannot give money, then here are some more things to keep in mind. Always be ready with your answer to a request for money, so you don't end up getting flustered and ignoring the human who is right there in front of you. Even giving someone just a smile and your attention for a few moments is far better than pretending they do not exist. Sometimes people will not be happy with that response to a request for money, but I've spoken to many people living on the streets who have told me that they would prefer someone being honest and acknowledging them than ignoring them or waving them off like a fly. Yes, that's how it feels. This is a person who deserves the same compassion we afford everyone else. Sometimes compassion means being honest about limitations and being kind enough to own your personal decision to not give out money to strangers.

But money is not the only material support you can give someone. If you have time, you can offer to buy someone a meal or some groceries. And you can always ask if there is anything else they need that you can buy them. You could carry gift cards for local restaurants or coffeeshops to give away as well. Those kinds of gift cards buy more than a hot beverage and a bite to eat. They also purchase a few priceless hours of protection from the elements.

Here's another great idea for a compassionate response to someone asking for help. Growing up in Cameroon, one of my best friends was a kid named Erik. He and his family were forced to move to Cameroon when the country they were serving in as missionaries devolved into civil war. Fast forward some 20 years and he and I are still in touch. He and his wife financially support my work at City Relief, and they even served with us for a week in 2020.

Erik reached out to me before their visit because he wanted to know what our policy was on kids volunteering at our outreaches. I told him that we can't bring someone to one of our events who's younger than 18 for liability reasons. He replied, "I thought I'd ask. My daughter Juliet has an obvious heart for the homeless. She's six years old. I figure this is too young for anything, but it's pretty incredible: She spots homeless folks everywhere and asks how she can help them. She prayed the other night that God would make a way for her to give them all houses and food."

I replied to Erik by telling him he's describing a future Outreach Leader at City Relief! I also told him that I know kids who have put together packages of travel-size hygiene supplies like deodorant, soap, toothpaste, toothbrushes, or new socks to have ready to go in case they happen to meet someone experiencing homelessness.

Later that same day, Erik texted me again. "Bro, Juliet didn't waste any time! Told me we *had* to get some stuff for what she's calling 'kindness kits.'"

ENGAGING NEIGHBORS WITH COMPASSION

If you carry supplies like these around in case you bump into someone who may need them, it's always important to ask first whether or not the person you're offering them to is even interested. It's not dignifying or compassionate to assume that someone who's asking for money needs a new pair of socks or a stick of deodorant. But in my experience, the vast majority of people you ask will be extremely appreciative of the gesture.

Just a few days after my text exchange with Eric, he reached out again: "My daughter gave away her first 'kindness kit' today. She made my wife turn around and go all the way back to give it to him. He was so grateful and she was thrilled! One thing that impacted her when she gave it to him was that he said, 'Thank you for talking to me.' Later on, she asked us what he meant by that. So, we explained that many people just walk by and ignore them."

Eric told me that she replied, "That's so sad! Don't people know they're people too?"

I think Juliet is the perfect example of what compassion looks like in action. We don't prepare socks or hygiene bags to keep in our cars or purses because homeless people need our pity. We don't form a plan and have an answer ready for the panhandler because we will feel bad if we don't. We do it for the simple reason that they're people too. They have intrinsic worth, and they have more to offer than most people believe.

It shouldn't surprise any of us that Marcus had the energy and willingness to jump up and spend all that time digging me out of that snowbank. As this book has hopefully made clear, homeless people are, probably more than anyone you know, survivors. The danger, the logistical complications, the stress, the ridicule, the stereotypes, the exclusion — it's more than most housed people ever have to handle. Remember James, my friend who believed I was an undercover FBI agent? That guy managed to survive for years with limited income, no support system, and significant delusions about the world around him. He found food, shelter, and clothing in a world that he believed to be even more hostile than it certainly is. That man was a survivor.

Recognizing the humanity of unhoused people involves taking seriously what they've been through. So I want to make one final, important point here. People will not always receive attempts at compassion as they are intended. If someone responds dismissively or angrily to you, try not to beat yourself up about it or take it personally. You never know exactly what's going on in someone's life. But you know it probably hasn't been easy. People living on the streets are often sleep-deprived. They've often been enduring judgment and hostility, so their emotional walls can be strategic. They may think your intentions are condescending or patronizing (and sometimes, they might be right!). Or they might just be having a bad day. Just remember: these are people. You don't help for any reason other than that. And you can only do what you can do. Compassion cannot be contingent on the receptivity of the person to whom you're offering it. True compassion is always based on what you're trying to demonstrate, regardless of how the person responds. By seeing the people all around you who might be lonely or in need, and by engaging them with a plan and a tangible expression of your concern for their humanity, you will make this world a little better one interaction at a time.

Going Further

I was in a hurry. I left a meeting with faith leaders at a church in Midtown Manhattan and wanted to get to Penn Station as quickly as possible to catch my train back home. My commute would depend on how fast I could get to the E train subway entrance, fight through the sea of people cascading into the station, wrestle my way onto a train, and then sprint through the underground maze of hallways and escalators in Penn Station to the correct track. It was just after 5:00 p.m., so the odds weren't in my favor.

I jogged down Fifth Avenue, crossed over East 53rd Street, sidestepped a delivery guy on a bicycle, and saw the subway entrance around the corner. As I entered the station, my prospects dimmed. It was packed. For a moment, I naïvely hoped that all those people might be going in a different direction than I was.

I walked toward the escalator that would take me to my platform. As I did, I noticed a woman in her 20s sitting on the floor to my left. She sat cross-legged with a cardboard sign in her lap that said, "Homeless and hungry, anything helps." The station was way too crowded for me to make eye contact, and the human current was too strong for me to stop and approach her. Before I knew it, I was on the escalator moving away from her and toward the downtown line. I decided there was nothing I could do, and turned to see if the platform I was moving toward was less crowded. I should have known better. I watched as an E train pulled up with people crammed inside like sardines, and there was no space for any of the growing crowd to climb aboard.

As I evaluated my options, I recalled the nice weather, and decided that walking the 20 blocks to Penn Station would be worth avoiding this nonsense. I pushed my way to the escalator going back up. The young lady who was panhandling upstairs was still on my mind. I was ready to push through the crowd toward her this time, and I was clearly no longer in a rush because rushing was no longer an option. I decided to stop and say hello. I mentally developed a plan as I approached her. I stepped out of the flow of pedestrians and up against the wall next to her, facing the same way she was.

"Hi there! How are you surviving this crowd?"

She was startled for a second that someone was standing next to her and speaking to her, but she recovered quickly. "I'm used to it."

Up close, I realized that she was even younger than I thought. She had blue eyes and blond hair that was pulled back into a ponytail. Her clothes were dirty, and she had two big bags of belongings that formed a wall around her.

"I was going to get a subway downtown, but that's not going to happen. Would you mind if I sat next to you for a few minutes and kept you company while I wait to see if this crowd thins out? I promise I won't stay long, and I'll try not to annoy you."

She smiled as she said, "Sure, have a seat."

I sat down next to her and for a few seconds we just watched the people continue to pour in and out of the station. It was an interesting perspective shift. I was now looking at people's legs as they rushed by, and I realized that this had been what she saw me do just a few moments before.

"My name is Josiah. What do your friends call you?"

"Katie."

"Nice to meet you, Katie. Are you making any money here or are people too rushed to stop?"

"I'm doing okay. I figure I need another 20 dollars to get some food and a metro card, and then I'll have enough."

"It's a beautiful day. I hope you get it soon so you can get out of here and go outside."

We continued talking for a few minutes about the weather and her experiences panhandling. But then Katie shared that she had a daughter. The girl lived with Katie's mother. Katie was trying to get her life together so that she and her daughter could reunite, but she kept falling back into addiction and abusive relationships.

"When was the last time you tried to get some help with your addiction?" I asked.

"Oh, I had a few months clean a year or two ago, but then I relapsed." She paused to say thank you to someone who dropped a few dollars in her cup. "I don't even know where to go for help anymore."

"Well, you may find this hard to believe, but I can help you with that."

"Really? How?"

I explained what City Relief does. I also pulled out my card and gave it to her. "Do you mind if I ask you a few personal questions?" Even though she had already voluntarily opened up to me about her life and her daughter, I always try not to presume.

"I don't mind."

"Cool. What are you using right now?"

"Heroin," she said.

"How much do you use? Do you take any prescription medication? Any alcohol?"

"I use about three or four bags a day depending on how much money I get. I was on psych meds, but I stopped taking them because my Medicaid was cut off and I couldn't see my doctor. I drink sometimes, but not a lot. Mostly it's just the heroin."

"Have you ever been to detox? Have you ever tried medication-assisted treatment like Suboxone or methadone?"

"No, not really."

"You said your Medicaid was cut off. Was it cut off or restricted? Do you know?"

"Nope. I have no idea. It just stopped working. But I have my benefits card right here." She reached into one of her bags.

"That's great! Do you mind if I take a picture of it with my phone so that my team can follow up and see if we can turn it back on?"

"No, I don't mind at all. That would be amazing!" I took a picture of the card and gathered some more personal information.

"Would you be interested in getting some help? I mean, if I could find you a place to go, and I could get your Medicaid back on, would you go?"

"Absolutely! I don't want to keep living like this."

"I don't blame you," I said. "So, let's do this. Do you have a phone?"

"Yeah." She pulled out an "Obama phone," free phones that people with limited financial resources can access through phone companies who have contracts with the federal government.

I called myself with her phone so that I would have her number and she would have mine. While I had my phone out, I searched for locations in the area where she could go for help at any time, and I wrote down their contact information on the back of my business card. We kept chatting for a few more minutes, but I decided that I had helped her as much as I could for the time being, and I didn't want to run the risk of overstaying my welcome. I thanked her for her time and her company, and I stood up to leave.

"Katie, I really believe you can have the life you've always dreamed of. You and your little girl can be together again. Can you try to be safe and maybe go to those places on the back of that card tomorrow?"

She started to tear up. "Yes. I can do that. Thank you."

"Thank you, Katie. My team will be calling you. Okay? We want to help however we can." Unfortunately, I can't tell you the end of Katie's story. Other outreach workers took her case after I made contact. But I tell you this story to demonstrate the kinds of interactions I want people to have, and introduce you to the kinds of things you are capable of doing yourself, whether you believe it or not.

As we've discussed, we should respond to our homeless neighbors with tangible things like cash, meals, clothing, and emergency supplies. This is a recognition of the simple fact that they're people too. But recognizing their humanity also means being ready to address the deeper challenges they face, as well as our collective human need for connection. Ever since my daughter was born, I have been thinking about interactions like the one with Katie differently; if I ever met Katie's parents and they asked me how I tried to help their daughter, I wouldn't want to only say that I gave her a new pair of socks or a few dollars. Simple acts of generosity are a necessary step in building trust. But they are only the first step in truly helping someone who's experiencing homelessness.

You do not have to be an expert to connect someone to resources and services that can change their lives. It's true that people in my line of work know more about services for people living on the streets than the average person. But nowadays almost everyone has a tool connecting them to all the information on the internet right in their pockets. I've spent years training and leading outreach leaders who work full time on the streets. I can't tell you how many times I have said "Google it" after one of them asked about a homeless person's problem that they couldn't solve. Most programs and resources have websites that include a phone number or an intake contact person. Just calling and asking some simple questions can get you a lot further than you might think.

Some people living on the street, like Katie, have access to cellphones. Some do not. But even for those who do, sometimes they just don't have the courage or the emotional bandwidth to call the places that they find when they search on the web. This is understandable given all we've discussed about the difficulty of living unhoused. Just having someone else do a little work can be an enormous gift.

But you don't need to wait for a specific person or problem to come along to begin researching. What if you researched the emergency shelter, rehab, or food pantry services in your community just to be ready when the need arises? You could even develop a resource guide for yourself to help those struggling with homelessness. What if you volunteered at the programs that you found so that you could talk about those places with a firsthand understanding of what they are like?

As you begin contacting organizations like these on behalf of your unhoused neighbors, you will run into an unfortunate truth. Many government programs, social services, or faith-based organizations have staff who are less patient with homeless guests than they are with people who have homes. In fact, one of the most common complaints I get from the people I have met in the street is that program staff who are supposed to help them often antagonize them instead. It isn't fair. It isn't right. But it's reality, and this is another problem you might be able to help solve.

One time I was sitting across the table from a new homeless friend named Carlos who didn't have a phone. He asked to use mine so he could call a caseworker at a shelter that he had recently left. He wanted to know if his personal belongings were still in his locker there, and if so, what time he could come in and collect them.

I dialed the number and put it on speaker. The person who answered the phone was argumentative and impatient. He wouldn't give a clear answer, so finally I spoke up.

"Excuse me, hello. My name is Josiah and I'm an outreach worker with an organization called City Relief. I'm sitting here with Carlos and I've been listening to the conversation. Really, all we need to know is if Carlos's stuff is still in his locker and, if so, what time can he come in today or tomorrow to collect it? I'd really appreciate your help. I understand there might be complications, but I'd be happy to help Carlos get there at a time that would be convenient for you."

It was like the person on the other end of the line was body snatched by a nice person. All of a sudden, he became clear, concise, and helpful. I got the information we needed and ended the call.

Carlos looked at me incredulously. "Can you call my doctor next?"

I'm not trying to stereotype the staff at shelters and social service organizations. Many of them are gracious and generous, patient and kind. But they're also often over worked and under paid, and they deal with a lot of stressful situations. Advocates for homeless people need to understand that and sometimes confront them accordingly.

Recently I was serving near a partner organization that does incredible things for their community. There was a security guard sitting outside their building while our outreach was going on. I was talking to one of our guests who was homeless who asked me if we had any clothes to give away. Specifically, he needed a pair of jeans with a size 38 waist. I didn't have any clothing with me so I started asking some locals if there were any nearby thrift or department stores. There wasn't. I walked up to the security guard to ask if the director of the program was inside.

He replied, "Yeah, but maybe I can help. What do you need?"

"I am talking to this guy over there at the table and he needs a pair of pants. You guys don't happen to have a pair of jeans size 38 do you?"

"That guy? Oh, that guy is a problem. I'll take care of it." He stood up and started to walk over to the table.

"Wait! He isn't a problem right now; he just needs pants. He's chilling. Do you have pants?" I was surprised at how fast the situation was escalating.

"You don't understand. That guy is cool one minute and crazy the next! He will scream and curse at people. I'll take care of this." The security guard was determined to engage.

"Hold on. Maybe that's true. But as of this moment, he is calm and sitting down with my staff. He is eating and happy. He has done nothing wrong! All I need to know is whether or not you have a pair of pants in your building that are size 38?"

"Are you sure? This guy…" I interrupted him.

"I'm sure. If he flips out, my team will deal with it. But for now, do you have any pants?"

"I think so." He turned around and went back into the building. He came back out five minutes later with a gray pair of jeans that were clean and folded.

"Thank you so much!" I took the jeans and walked them over to the guest at our table. He graciously thanked me and I pointed to the security guard and said, "Actually, he gave them to you." The security guard waved and smiled.

Unfortunately, many people who work in environments where there are lots of unhoused people end up viewing the people their job exists to help as enemies to be contained. Sometimes having an outsider simply demonstrate an interest in helping someone get from point A to point B can make a huge difference by reminding the staff or the volunteers who may or may not be tired and burnt out why their job exists in the first place. These situations can be difficult, and you may not navigate them perfectly right away. But never assume that you have nothing to offer because you don't understand the system or the process. You can make a difference by simply being present and doing whatever you can to get people what they need.

Now this may sound obvious, but getting people what they need requires knowing what they need. To do that most effectively, you have to form connections with people and ask good questions. Connection always begins with a conversation. One question I like to lead with is simply, "I live in New Jersey, so I'm not a true New Yorker. What about you? Have you lived in New York City for a long time?" The answer you get will tell you a lot.

For example, when I was speaking to Katie in the subway station, if I had asked her whether she lived in New York City for a long time and she said yes, I could have easily followed up with a question about where specifically? Or, if she had said "No, I just moved here," I could have asked what brought her to the city? Then I could have followed up with something like, "Do you like it here?" Either way, gently showing interest in where someone passes most of their time and how they feel about it could open the door for them to share a status update on their journey: what they're doing, how they got there, and where they want to be. I've found that most people living on the streets are completely willing to share some version of their story. If we're going to foster any significant connection with our homeless neighbors, we need to start by showing interest in their lives.

Sometimes less common, open-ended questions are another way to find out what if anything someone needs. I sometimes use some version of this one: If you could change one thing about your life, what would that be? Mark Horvath, founder of the advocacy group Invisible People, likes to ask, "If you had three wishes, what would they be?" Both questions accomplish the same purpose. they give a person who may be struggling with some big issues a clear opportunity to disclose what their most urgent challenge is and what they believe would fix it. But if they're not ready to disclose that, these questions still let you demonstrate interest and give you the chance to learn something interesting.

Asking questions is also important to avoid making assumptions. Another time I was talking with a guy that I met at Penn Station. A woman approached us from the crowd and very directly and rudely said to my new friend, "My church gives out food to the homeless every Thursday. You should come."

I was expecting him to reply with a colorful version of "Take a hike," because that's what I wanted to say. My new friend was far more gracious than I would have been. He thanked her for her concern, and then explained that he had enough food to eat, and that he was not in fact homeless.

That story is an extreme example, but hopefully it gets the point across: don't assume. I have made the mistake of thinking I knew what someone living on the street needs, only to have them realize that the service I offered them isn't the right fit and walk out the door.

If someone shares with you what they want to change about their lives, try asking how they've tried to accomplish that already. What worked in the past, what didn't, and why? We should not assume that what worked for one person will work for everyone. For instance, I've tried connecting cigarette smokers who wanted to get free from heroin to rehab programs where they're not allowed to smoke. It didn't always work. But sometimes it did. Asking someone to give up heroin and nicotine simultaneously is unbelievably difficult. Some are ready to try. Others aren't. Want to know how to tell the difference? Ask!

Connecting with people in the ways I've outlined here is how to move beyond simple acts of compassion. This connection is the difference between helping someone survive today and helping them thrive tomorrow. It's the missing link between transactional charity and holistic engagement. All it takes is intentionality. You don't have to be an expert. You just have to care and put in the work.

Building Community

I met Sunny a long time ago in Manhattan. He and his friend Jake would often stop by our outreach locations just to check in and say hello. Sunny is an older gentleman who moved from Vietnam to the States as a child. He never received a Social Security number, so he has never had state identification. Consequently, he has always had trouble finding work. He was living on the street, and many people had tried over the years to take advantage of his soft, open heart (not to mention his small stature). But none of this ever seemed to dampen his mood or his optimism. He was always smiling at anyone he passed on the subway or the street. And Sunny always had Jake.

Jake is a middle-aged white man who also found himself sleeping on the streets. Jake was much more guarded. While Sunny operated with an unending supply of hope, Jake survived by sleeping with one eye open. Jake would normally crash on the steps of an old church in Midtown. While Jake and Sunny didn't always stay together, every time I saw one of them, the other wasn't too far off. They reminded me a little of Bert and Ernie from *Sesame Street*.

I would always offer them whatever supplies I could collect, and I repeatedly tried to help them get indoors. Sunny was never interested. Like many of our homeless neighbors, he had some bad experiences in shelters. Jake was totally comfortable outside throughout most of the year but occasionally allowed me to refer him to an emergency shelter when the weather was really bad. These two had figured out a way to survive, and the only options that I could give them were never appealing enough to motivate long-term change. Then Covid hit. I saw Sunny at our Chelsea Park outreach in March of 2020 and, as usual, he gave me a big smile.

"Josiah! Good news. Jake is house sitting for someone who's out of the country, and I found a room that I can stay in for $250 a month!" This was huge. In nine years, I had never known either of them to stay indoors for any substantial period of time, but the falling rent and the empty city homes of the pandemic created opportunities for them. Sunny told me that he needed peanut butter, jelly, and bread so he could stay indoors and quarantine. I assured him I would make it happen. When we were back at Chelsea Park the following week, I showed up with the supplies. Sunny gave me a huge hug and thanked me profusely for the groceries. Then, unsurprisingly, he disappeared. I didn't think anything of it because I knew that he was indoors.

In March of 2021, I was at our 14th Street outreach location, and there he was. He looked terrible. He was barely able to crack a smile for me. He was unshaven and he looked skinny and pale.

"Sunny! How are you?"

"Not so good, Josiah. I was diagnosed with diabetes last fall. And two weeks ago I lost my room, so I've been sleeping on cardboard on 31st Street."

"Is Jake still housesitting?"

"Oh, yes. Jake is doing very well." The idea of Sunny sleeping on a piece of cardboard on 31st Street all by himself made me ache. Sunny was picking at his soup.

"Is the soup okay?" I asked.

"Oh, yes. It's fine. I just can't eat the rice. So, I'm picking out the beans and the vegetables."

"Would you like me to get you a cup with just broth?" I was desperate to help in some tangible way.

"No. No, Josiah. It's okay."

"Sunny, you don't look so good. Can I put you up in a hotel for a few nights?" I couldn't imagine my friend sleeping another night on cardboard. With his health issues and his temperament, he was an obvious target. Sunny agreed to the offer, and my team and I were able to get him into an Uber to take him directly to a room where he could rest for a few nights while we tried to advocate for a better long-term solution.

I sent my colleague a text message that said, "We need to do something for my friend Sunny. I have known him for years and he's truly one of my favorites. Just to put it in perspective, I'm not a hugger, but I always hug Sunny."

A few days later, I received an email from an outreach worker from another organization who said they were also trying to get Sunny placed as soon as possible. Because he was in a hotel, we had a few extra days to get the documentation he needed together, and within a few days Sunny was in a room that he could stay in for the long haul. I was thrilled. I called Sunny a few days later to check on him and make sure he was doing alright.

"Josiah, I have a microwave and a minifridge! I have everything I need!"

Once you have been able to tangibly offer compassion and connection, the next step in recognizing the humanity of your unhoused neighbors is building community with them. Sunny is a friend of mine. Over time, step by step, I built a relationship with him. I know his friends, and he knows mine. I helped him with a variety of things over the years. And I certainly can't afford to put just anyone up in a hotel. If my family had had room, I would have just taken Sunny home when I heard he was sleeping on the street.

Unfortunately, too many people approach serving their homeless neighbors with the belief that those neighbors are charity cases. Building community and friendships with your neighbors can help break down that pattern of thinking and lead to more real, humane connections between people. This includes honoring the autonomy of your neighbors the way you would any friend, even if you think you would make different choices than they do. For years, I offered Sunny connections to services but I had to be okay with him saying, "No, thanks." If we try to build a community where homeless folks are welcomed and loved, we cannot think of them as projects.

And if they are not projects, then we will create opportunities for them to positively participate in community, instead of exclusively being recipients of aid. If you don't intentionally make these opportunities, you may send the message that you think homeless people are fundamentally less valuable.

One of my best friends is named Aaron. As I write this, he's bouncing back and forth between living on the Appalachian Trail, in a friend's garage, and in a boarding house. I caught up with Aaron a few months back, and he told me about a recent time when he went to a food pantry in search of supplies.

He noticed that the volunteers and staff seemed to be overwhelmed, so he offered to help them out.

"The woman took one look at me and said, 'Sorry, you can't volunteer because you're a client.'" As Aaron recounted this story, he was visibly frustrated and said, "I just wanted to f*cking contribute!"

I took that story back with me to City Relief and we started an internship program so that our guests could volunteer *with* us, not just receive our services. City Relief, very fortunately, usually has an abundance of volunteers, but that can make it impossible for our guests to serve. We intentionally designed this program to make space in our standard operating procedures for those receiving services and resources from us to experience volunteering. These interns are now part of the team. We also provide them with fare for the subway and a phone because people living on the street are often excluded from community by transportation costs or a lack of technology.

Any organization or community that wants to address homelessness has to include a strategic effort like this to incorporate people like Sunny, Jake, and Aaron into its day-to-day activities. It takes intentionality. It will not happen by accident.

It's worth it, but doing this will always be challenging for at least two major reasons. First, society has trained many people in your community to ignore unhoused people's experiences and problems, and to assume the worst of them. Some people you know will be rude, impatient, or just plain ignorant around your homeless friends. But being candid with those homeless friends ahead of time about the people who might cause problems can help you build trust right out of the gate. Sadly, most people who experience homelessness are well aware of how others perceive them. So your warnings will help build trust, but they probably won't be a surprise. And if your homeless friend decides they don't want to deal with difficult people like that at the moment, you know what to do: respect their autonomy, and let them go. You will also want to start doing what you can to educate the people in your community about having a more compassionate outlook.

Second, opening up your life to people experiencing homelessness will create social situations you've probably never experienced before, so you will need to plan carefully, minimize the number of assumptions you make, and practice clear communication. You can do this by asking one simple question over and over again: then what?

Let's say you become friends with an unhoused neighbor and you want to invite them to use your shower. Then what? What if they aren't used to having privacy and a hot shower, so they take much longer than you expect? Do they have clean clothes to wear afterward? What if they finish and don't leave for a while? Is everyone in your home comfortable inviting them in? Will they be comfortable around everyone in your home? What if they keep asking if they can use your shower when they see you in the neighborhood? What if they ask if they can stay at your place for a while? Then what?

Maybe you want to let a homeless friend get out of some bad weather by sitting in your office. Then what? Is there any chance someone will need the room your friend is sitting in? Is there someone whose permission you need to use a room this way? Is there anyone in the office who might complain? How often should you go and check on your friend? What if the weather stays bad past the end of the workday? Then what?

The answer to "Then what?" is not always easy and will depend on your circumstances. You need to practice telling people your expectations in a kind, compassionate way, keeping in mind that the response may not always be positive. But that's alright. In the long run, understanding and communicating your capacity will help avoid burnout and maintain friendships.

All this may sound hard, but I don't mean to deter you from helping your neighbors. I want to help you avoid situations for which you are unprepared so that those situations don't become barriers to community and relationships — or so that you don't become disoriented or frustrated and do or say things you might regret later.

Beyond asking the question "then what," we need to intentionally build ways to incorporate our homeless neighbors into our communal lives. And we need to take seriously the challenges they face. We need to talk to our coworkers, faith communities, and families about the realities of homelessness and how we can work together to be aware, strategic, and responsive. If you live, work, or play in areas that have a larger population of homeless folks, develop a plan. Who will take the responsibility of engaging with them in conversations that offer connections to relationships and resources? How can you collectively invest your time, your talent, and your treasure to see and advocate for your homeless neighbors?

I have a friend named Bindia who started volunteering with City Relief at the peak of the pandemic in 2020. She enthusiastically served for an hour or so before asking me if we were safe in the Harlem community where we set up. I smiled and told her that we were no less safe than we would be walking from point A to point B in any other part of the city. She accepted that answer and continued to show up. Week after week, she was there.

Bindia started bringing supplies from home to give out to our homeless guests. Even more importantly, she invited friends to come along — work friends, church friends, and neighbors — anyone she could think of who might be inspired by the opportunity to give back. Along the way, she and I continued to have conversations about homelessness and how our work was designed to empower change in the lives of those we serve. She told me about a vision she had for a project that she called "Adopt a Grandad."

"You know, there are so many older homeless people who don't seem to have anyone in their lives. It's just so wrong. I'd like to start something where families can 'adopt' someone elderly and be his family. I even have the perfect person who I want to start with. His name is John. I met him at Chelsea Park. He's the kindest, sweetest man. He's in his late 70s, and I cannot bear to see him live another day on the street!"

At the time, I responded with what I hoped was realistic optimism. "That sounds great, Bindia! Let's keep praying and see what happens!"

A few months later, Bindia reached out to me again. "Josiah, I just saw John at Chelsea Park! I hadn't seen him in a while, and I was so worried. But he's back, and he's willing to consider coming inside! I introduced him to the city outreach workers who showed up at City Relief, and they told me that they have been trying to get John indoors for 20 years, but he won't talk to them!"

"Wow! That's amazing!" I didn't know John, and I didn't know what the options would look like. But Bindia was determined, and I really wanted to fan the flames of her optimism. Just a few days later she reached out again.

"I'm in a cab with John and I'm taking him to transitional housing on the East Side!"

"Seriously?" I was in awe of her compassion and her determination. "'Adopt a Grandad' is really happening!"

Over the next few weeks, I watched from a distance as Bindia, her husband, her son, her neighbors, and even her doorman all got involved in John's life. Not only is Bindia helping him get to and from his appointments and making sure that his caseworkers are moving his housing applications forward, she's also allowing John to spend time with her family in her home.

At one point, John left his new housing placement and got lost, because it was in a new neighborhood with which he was unfamiliar. He ended up wandering the streets for three days until Bindia miraculously found him near Times Square. She transported him back to his housing placement and helped him use a cellphone that she got him so that he could always reach out for help if he needed it. Bindia was later able to connect John to a long-term housing facility just a few blocks from her home. There he can come and go as he pleases. And he receives wraparound services from a team of people who are all working with Bindia to make sure that John has access to both the resources and the community that he needs.

Bindia started off being worried about the safety of volunteering on the street. Less than a year later, she was leading the way for others like her to create real, restorative community with unhoused people. But her story is not unique. Building a community response to homelessness almost always starts with one person taking their knowledge and experience, asking questions about the real needs of individuals who are their friends, and finding thoughtful and compassionate ways to integrate those individuals into their lives. Don't let the enormity of the society-wide problems stop you. We all need to start small with people we personally know, and grow from there. Hopefully, this book has given you a framework to do just that, and now you can look for the beginning of your personal path to start the work.

Bringing It Home

This book only scratches the surface of what leads someone in America to live without stable housing. Homelessness is like an ocean where all the rivers of poverty and streams of injustice pool together when they're allowed to flow undeterred. I have spent the last decade of my life trying to pull people out of the waves, while other organizations and individuals are upstream trying to stop or slow the current of each individual issue. Those currents include the affordable housing crisis, economic injustice, systemic racism, discriminatory policing and court systems, domestic violence, poor mental health treatment, substance addiction, the foster care system, and everything in between. But the complexity of the problems also means that there's a starting point for anyone who wants to get involved.

If you don't know where to start, I'd suggest volunteering your time with an organization that's already involved in caring for the homeless community. Like I mentioned earlier, I didn't plan on working in this field. I started by washing dishes at a soup kitchen, and that led to serving in the streets with City Relief. Volunteering is one of the best ways to learn what you feel called to do. If you've never volunteered with a soup kitchen, a shelter, or a clothing bank, you should definitely give it a try. Don't set the bar too high for yourself. Just sign up for one event. Your first stop may not be your landing spot. Feel free to "shop around" for volunteer opportunities that allow you to leverage your strengths. There are lots of entry-level volunteer positions at nonprofit organizations. You don't have to make a big splash to make a difference!

Another route to getting started that I've seen many people take is to mobilize their friends and family. You can get people to sign up and volunteer with you, or to help you organize a food, clothing, or toiletry drive. You can head out into the streets as a group and distribute these items yourselves, or you can find an organization that will distribute them for you. You can talk to them about investing financially in organizations doing work you all admire. Or you could come up with your own creative way to serve based on the needs of the people you know in your neighborhood.

You may not be the kind of person who is passionate about volunteering on the front lines to directly serve people experiencing homelessness. There are still so many ways for you to get involved and leverage your talents and your resources to improve lives. Consider offering to help organizations in areas like finance, human resources, web or graphic design, IT, or whatever your area of expertise might be. So many nonprofits have to choose between allocating finite resources directly into programming for the marginalized and hurting, or into their own infrastructure. The urgency of the needs of the people they serve often end up superseding their organizational needs, which are still critical, if less immediate. Your skills and your investment couldn't be more necessary.

I met Tommy years ago when I first moved to New Jersey. He was involved in a religious group for college students that I led with my wife. Fast forward 10 years and Tommy is married with kids and works for a multibillion-dollar company as an expert in analyzing healthcare plans at a very high level. City Relief was struggling to keep up with our healthcare costs at one point and Tommy volunteered his time to sort through our options and come up with a plan that was both comprehensive and affordable. As a specialist, his time also counted as a valuable in-kind donation to our organization.

Reach out to organizations in your community that are helping to improve the lives of the homeless and the marginalized and offer to spend a day fixing, building, driving, or using your skills for whatever they need. I guarantee that they will gladly accept your offer and will probably invite you back when they need your help again.

You never know how skills you have might be of assistance. City Relief, for instance, is always on the lookout for volunteers who have Commercial Driver's Licenses to help us get our supplies, staff, and volunteers from our base of operations to the outreach locations where we serve. When we're low on drivers, volunteers have stepped up and single-handedly enabled us to serve hundreds of people at a time.

You can also use your expertise by teaching others what you know. Helping individuals experiencing homelessness learn trades and skills that will allow them to make a living is vital work. And you are only fully utilizing your skills if you are sharing them with others.

I would also suggest being intentional about where you spend your money. Some for-profit companies use their revenue and commodities in fantastic ways to help unhoused people. For example, City Relief has an incredible relationship with the apparel company, Bombas. They donate one pair of highly durable and comfortable socks to nonprofits who serve the unhoused community for every pair that they sell. So there are ways to help your neighbors even while doing something as mundane as buying yourself socks.

Maybe you're an activist who wants to see policy changes at local, state, and federal levels. I'm convinced this is God's work. My friends at Human.nyc, VOCAL-NY, the Urban Justice Center, the Legal Aid Society, Coalition for the Homeless, and many others are literally saving lives by speaking up and forcing systemic change. But they always need volunteers to create momentum and political will. You could also attend community board meetings and speak up on behalf of those who are unable or not allowed to speak up for themselves. Learn about different proposals that people are putting forward in your communities and ask the hard questions about how these policies will impact homeless residents. You can show up and document what is happening when the police take action around a tent community or homeless shelter. You can write letters or call your representatives, and you can share articles about homeless issues on social media.

The problem of homelessness is too big for any single person or organization to tackle alone. But we should never let the size and scope of the problem stop us from doing something about it. One of my favorite quotes is from Bishop Desmond Tutu. He says, "If you are neutral in situations of injustice, you have chosen the side of the oppressor. If an elephant has its foot on the tail of a mouse and you say that you are neutral, the mouse will not appreciate your neutrality." There are homeless people all around us who have the elephant feet of entire economic, social, and political systems on their tails. The question is: what are you willing to do about it?

My Neighbors

It has been my goal from the start of this book to remind us of the people behind the politics and public policy of homelessness. To that end, I reached out to some of my friends who have been or are currently unhoused. I asked them if they'd be willing to let me tell their stories and hire a photographer to take their portraits in an attempt to highlight the dignity and the individuality of their experiences. It is with great pride that I get to share with you the following images and stories of my friends who remind me every day why I do what I do.

NEIGHBORS WITH NO DOORS

Mady was born in Paris, France. His entire family is from the Ivory Coast, but he and his mother moved to New York City in 1982 when he was a kid. Eventually they ended up in Memphis, Tennessee. Mady says that he experienced incredible racism and discrimination there when he was young, so he decided to move back to New York City on his own as soon as possible.

When he arrived, he managed to get a good job that paid well, but he made what he describes as some wrong turns along the way and started drinking and partying a lot. This led to him losing his job, and without any family or community to turn to, he ended up on the streets. In 2010, he entered a residential program for homeless men in Lower Manhattan to try to rebuild his life, but it didn't stick.

When I met Mady for the first time many years ago he was back on the street. Because of my background in Cameroon and my French, I was able to connect with him right away. We became friends almost instantly, and when Covid-19 hit New York City and everything shut down, City Relief was able to get him a phone and some connections to resources to help him stabilize. Now Mady is in a shelter in the Bronx, and while he continues to meet us on the streets, it's mostly because we're his community, not because he needs our help. I asked him what motivates him to keep fighting for his future, and he replied, "I want to bless other people!"

NEIGHBORS WITH NO DOORS

MY NEIGHBORS

Hakki is one of the most famous formerly homeless people I know. He has been featured in *the New York Times*, in *Forbes*, and on *NBC News*. He was born in a remote village in Turkey where he ended his education early to make money for his family by selling cigarettes, matches, and candles on the street. As a teenager his parents sent him to Montreal to work in his brother's pizza shop. At the age of 21, he got a one-way bus ticket to New York City to chase the American dream, but quickly learned it's a dream that is easier for some to achieve than others. After a week, all his money was gone and he was sleeping in Grand Central Station. He found his way to the Bowery Mission's facility in Lower Manhattan where he lived in a residential program for about three months while he pursued his career as a "pizza guy." He managed to save up enough money to buy a tiny pizzeria. He wasn't making any money until he caught a break in 2010 by winning a large pizza-making contest. He then opened seven stores in five years, and now the Champion Pizza chain and his rags-to-riches story are both well known.

I met him in 2020 at the height of the Covid-19 pandemic. While we were serving food to men and women outside of the Bowery Mission, he approached me and asked who we were. While I was explaining, I said that everyone was telling us we all have to stay home. But what do you do if you have no home? he got really excited and pulled out his phone. "Can you say that again?" I learned later that he has millions of followers on social media and he spends a lot of his time advocating and giving back to people who are going through exactly what he experienced.

Hakki is also my first call if we happen to run out of food at a City Relief outreach because he immediately contacts one of his stores and has them make as many pizzas as we need for our guests.

NEIGHBORS WITH NO DOORS

MY NEIGHBORS

I met Eric briefly at an outreach event a few years back. It was raining and cold. He was homeless and struggling with alcoholism. I spoke to him about his living situation and connected him to a program that would help him with some problems he was having receiving his food stamps. A year later, he walked into another outreach and I found out that he was still trying to find his way to some stability. He also said he had been arrested out of state. He wasn't charged with a crime, but the time he had spent in jail lost him his bed. I was able to connect him to a program in a partner organization that allowed him to stabilize and helped him get a job with the New York City Metro Transit Authority.

He recently returned to one of our outreaches looking for me because he wanted to say thank you for the help that he had received. He's now working full time and has maintained his sobriety for over a year. He told my co-worker, "You know, sometimes help doesn't look like help. But Josiah gave me some simple directions and I was able to follow through and get what I needed. I graduated from the program and went back to school. When the pandemic came, I thought my life was over. But thanks to Josiah, I was an essential worker so I worked every day of the pandemic! I am no longer homeless because I encountered City Relief!"

NEIGHBORS WITH NO DOORS

I was doing some work on my computer at an outreach one day while one of my colleagues spoke with Elijah about some resources he needed. He was sleeping in Central Park at the time and dealing with severe depression. Something drew me into their conversation. I wandered over and sat down next to them. My wife and I were planning on going to a gospel choir concert the next evening in Harlem, and I thought maybe he could use the encouragement and the community. I invited him to meet us there.

When the concert started, he hadn't arrived, and I was disappointed. But five minutes into the show he walked in. I jumped over the people sitting next to me to get to him and brought him back to his reserved seat. Since then, his life has had its ups and downs. He was one of the first people that City Relief brought into our internship program in 2020. We got him off the streets and into a shelter bed for a while. We then worked to have him moved to a hotel room when the pandemic hit the city. He ended up contracting a very serious case of Covid-19 anyway and found himself on a ventilator in the hospital for several weeks.

When he recovered, our team was able to keep supporting him and we connected him to an organization where he found employment. Today, Elijah is housed and making a living. He is still living with depression. It's never easy, and I am honored to know Elijah as he continues to fight for his future.

NEIGHBORS WITH NO DOORS

I told Brian's story in the chapter on lies about laziness. He's the man who walked over 2 hours from Newark to City Relief headquarters. I instantly liked him. He was funny and honest. After the story I told, his past caught up with him again and he ended up back in jail.

In 2021 I pulled into the driveway of the City Relief base of operations, and Brian happened to be sitting on the sidewalk waiting for BJ, another one of our outreach team leaders. I gave him a big hug. We started talking, and I asked him what his plan was.

"Josiah, BJ is taking me to New York City where I'll get into the shelter system. But I'll need something to do! You know I need to work!"

Brian and I spoke about the City Relief internship program. He agreed to give it a try. Almost one year later, Brian completed the program and he just recently located an apartment that he can afford! Transitioning out of homelessness is rarely linear, but Brian is a constant reminder to me how friendship is often the most secure safety net anyone can have.

NEIGHBORS WITH NO DOORS

Charles approached me at one of our outreaches and asked if we had any way to help him get some clothing. It was winter and he needed a coat. An unfortunate truth for some low-income people is that men don't donate their clothing nearly as often as women do. This is why any given thrift store in America has a women's section that is much more robust than the men's. But the vast majority of unhoused people are men. At the time, I told him we didn't have anything in his size but that I was going to post the need on social media and see what I could come up with. A day later, my mother-in-law reached out to me and said that she wanted to donate $200 to help Charles get new clothing!

I ordered what he needed and delivered the items to him a week later. He was also in a terrible living situation and needed an advocate to help him communicate with his case worker. Soon after that, Charles also agreed to give our City Relief internship a try. He volunteered with us regularly, and really enjoyed chatting with our staff, particularly about American history. He also started working on his health, which he continued after he completed the internship. He gave up fried foods and started to play basketball again. Unfortunately, he fell and hurt his knee and his back. But even while injured, he kept trying to live a healthier lifestyle. Today, he's in a much better housing situation and we still communicate via Facebook Messenger on a regular basis.

MY NEIGHBORS

You already know Sunny. He's one of my favorite people. He has a home for the first time in many years. With his diabetes diagnosis, he's always using his smartphone to research what foods he should or shouldn't eat. He walks a lot and continues to stay as healthy as possible. He told me recently that he thinks the subways are more dangerous than they have been in years, so he tries to avoid them. Having spent many years homeless in Midtown Manhattan, that's where he spends his time when he's not in his room. The familiarity makes him feel safe.

Since we were able to help him get off the street, we are now working to help him access food that is good for his health, but also enjoyable. Sunny proudly told me that he got his Covid-19 vaccine as soon as he could, and he's grateful to not be sleeping on 31st Street anymore.

NEIGHBORS WITH NO DOORS

MY NEIGHBORS

This is John. You remember him — Bindia's "adopted" grandad. His story of transformation will go down as one of the most miraculous that I have witnessed. As a direct result of his work, along with Bindia's and her community's efforts, he's now in a long-term housing facility just a few blocks from her apartment and thriving after decades on the street. His ability to trust Bindia, and both of their determination to change his circumstances, is evidence of the power of community.

John was also the first person I asked to read this book from the perspective of someone who has experienced homelessness firsthand. His feedback was encouraging and insightful. He is so smart, funny, and kind, and his life looks more different than he could have thought possible even just months ago.

NEIGHBORS WITH NO DOORS

MY NEIGHBORS

Wayne was a professional musician for years. He traveled the world on cruise ships playing the bass for every kind of band imaginable. He's originally from London, England, and his accent, combined with his education, make him one of the most interesting and enjoyable conversationalists I have ever had the privilege of knowing.

I met him when he was going through one of the toughest seasons of his life. He had suffered a hand injury that caused nerve damage and made it impossible for him to play music. He had also gotten into a big argument with his wife that escalated to the point where he shoved her. He lost his housing and his marriage all at once. He says that it was his anger that led him to the streets.

He has been rebuilding ever since. During the Covid-19 pandemic, he tested positive for the virus. He was asymptomatic, and placed in an isolation hotel where he stayed for about a month before being transferred to a shelter in Brooklyn. After that, he was moved to a hotel in Manhattan where he has stayed for several months. He's working and saving money. He's also been able to get surgery on his hand that will hopefully allow him to regain the nerve sensitivity he needs to play music. I met with him recently and he told me his ability to stay positive hangs on his faith in God.

NEIGHBORS WITH NO DOORS

MY NEIGHBORS

We're going to end this book right where we started. This is Detra. She is my hero. You remember she moved to New York City when her marriage of over 30 years to an emotionally abusive pastor fell apart. When she found herself walking on the side of that highway without any idea of what to do next, a good Samaritan pulled over to offer her a ride. That one encounter changed everything.

When her housing difficulties started in New York City, she was working at Starbucks, but wasn't making enough money to pay rent. The former chairman of the board of a City Relief partner organization reached out to me because he met Detra through an acquaintance, but his organization wasn't equipped to work with her unique circumstances. Many shelters and programs unfortunately require time commitments and curfews that make it impossible to accommodate someone who's working odd hours. Detra was stuck. She and I met at one of the shelters that I knew was piloting a work program that allowed homeless people to stay indoors as long as they stayed employed. My colleague and I cried as we listened to Detra's heartbreaking story of abuse and neglect. We got her into the shelter/work program and connected her with some ongoing counseling services. Detra did the rest.

She kept working on herself and on her career. Nothing was going to stop her. She started boxing, networking, and even performing a one-woman show she wrote on stages around Manhattan. She found a new, full time, better paying job through talking to one of her customers at Starbucks. She even gave a TEDx talk in Europe about her experiences. She now rents her own apartment in New York City and is writing a book.

Acknowledgments

This book is for anyone who recognizes that human beings living in the wealthiest country of the world with no sustainable housing reflects badly on all of us. While I write these pages from the comfort of my own home, I hope my experiences and observations will humanize and amplify the voices of the real experts: those living on the streets.

I am so grateful for each person I have had the privilege of meeting in the streets of New York City and New Jersey. I would like to thank those who generously allowed me to use their names and photographs for this project, as well as the people who anonymously contributed their stories and their feedback. They inspire me every day and this book would be worthless without their input and their guidance.

I want to thank Corey Hayes for his masterful photography of my friends who I highlighted at the end of this book. He captured both their beauty and the depth of strength and resilience each one of them represents.

I am extremely grateful for the professional support and editing I received from Sy Hoekstra without whom this book would not exist. In addition to transforming my ramblings into coherent thoughts, Sy has been a wonderful coach and thought partner along the way.

I also need to thank everyone who I have had the privilege of working with at City Relief over the years. There are too many individuals to list, but I wouldn't be here without the perpetual support of colleagues, volunteers, board members, and advocates who compassionately serve their neighbors with no doors week in and week out. Whether I named you in this book or not, please know that you are on every single page.

Lastly, and most importantly, while I ran around the streets of New York and New Jersey over the last decade, my wife and kids cheered me on every step of the way. I would have nothing of substance to offer on this topic without their steadfast love and support of what I do. I am eternally grateful for their belief in me and their willingness to come with me on this incredible journey, even when that occasionally means I don't make it home for dinner.

Josiah Haken is the Chief Executive Officer of City Relief, a non-profit organization dedicated to connecting the unhoused community in New York City and New Jersey to resources that can change their lives. Each year, he manages hundreds of outreach and follow-up care efforts, involving thousands of volunteers. Josiah grew up as the son of missionaries in Yaoundé, Cameroon and has worked in the streets of New York City since 2010. These experiences give Josiah a unique perspective on the complexities of urban poverty, and he believes that our homeless neighbors deserve our best, not just our leftovers.

Josiah is widely recognized as a "go-to person" in New York City when it comes to teaching others how to engage with unhoused people. He leads workshops for many non-profit organizations and faith communities across the US. He is also one of the leading strategists for Don't Walk By, a series of homeless outreach events that mobilize thousands of volunteers and dozens of organizations throughout the month of February every year.

Josiah graduated from Fresno Pacific University with his M.A. in Ministry, Leadership, and Culture. His proudest accomplishments are deepening City Relief's ability to connect the people served with the resources needed to give them a fresh start, as well as consistently maintaining a perfect foam-to-milk ratio on an extra dry cappuccino. Find him on Twitter at @josiahhaken and on Instagram at @josiah_haken

Made in the USA
Columbia, SC
22 August 2022